TWENTY-ONE
YEARS YOUNG

TWENTY-ONE YEARS YOUNG

ESSAYS

AMY DONG

NEW DEGREE PRESS

COPYRIGHT © 2020 AMY DONG

All rights reserved.

TWENTY-ONE YEARS YOUNG

Essays

ISBN   978-1-63676-503-7   *Paperback*

          978-1-63676-019-3   *Kindle Ebook*

          978-1-63676-020-9   *Ebook*

For Mom, Dad, and Elaine.

妈, 爸, 这本书是为你们而写的。

Eli, in writing this, I hope I am now one step closer to becoming your Vincent Van Gogh.

CONTENTS

———

"At the core of the personal essay is the supposition that there is a certain unity to human experience."

—PHILLIP LOPATE,

THE ART OF THE PERSONAL ESSAY

"You are so young ... be patient toward all that is unsolved in your heart and to try to love the questions themselves like locked rooms and like books that are written in a very foreign tongue ... Live everything. Live the questions now. Perhaps you will then gradually, without noticing it, live along some distant day into the answer."

—RAINER MARIA RILKE,

LETTERS TO A YOUNG POET

INTRODUCTION

———

By the time this book of personal essays is published, I will have completed my final semester as an undergraduate student at New York University. College, for me, has been a period of overwhelming uncertainty punctured with moments of fleeting clarity. Of my four years at NYU, only two of them were spent in New York. The other two were spent doing things one rarely expects to be doing: living across twenty-five countries, recovering from an eating disorder, and penning a collection of essays in the midst of a global pandemic. I joined four dance teams and taught myself ukulele along the way—but only because I have never been good at sitting still.

As I close out seventeen years of classroom education, I find myself teetering on the edge of adulthood—young and confused, eager and impatient, and still quite naïve. In confessing these feelings in writing, I aim to impose some structure to it all. With writing as my magnifying lens, I hope to bring into focus the person I have become and the person I may one day be.

To that end, this book is a collection of essays about my life chosen for how deeply they have influenced my present ideals. I would like to tell you they all have to do with one

central theme, like uncertainty or youth or the loss of innocence, but that would be misleading. It would be more honest
simply to tell you they all reflect how I *feel*. They are novice
attempts to find individual meaning in the context of a larger
world; they are intensely personal searches for coherence
amidst confusion. Collected sporadically and accidentally
over the past two decades, these stories form a loose narrative
timeline for my life: the larger story at stake.

As young adults, we live, as always, in uncertain times.
We may feel that our current problems are unprecedented,
but of course they are not. Only our context has changed,
and to understand any of it, we must first understand ourselves. Thankfully, we are more competent at the latter than
we are often led to believe. We may only be twenty years old,
but two decades of living is not nothing: it is everything we
know. From fulfilling promises to falling out of love, from
discovering confidence to rediscovering faith, from com-
muning with failure to chasing after ephemeral joy—each of
our lives is already a colorful palimpsest of stories to reflect
on and to share.

The older we get, the more complex our lives become.
As our futures turn labyrinthine, the best way to navigate
them will be to spin stories the way Theseus spun his thread—
heading toward the unknown while safeguarding the past.
In my own unpredictable life, storytelling has been both a
dependable guide forward and a patient warden of everything left behind.

I found myself fully embracing the power of storytelling
during my last semester of college in an advanced writing
course called The Art of the Personal Essay. It was the only
course I took that year that was not part of the required business school curriculum. Of course, it was also my favorite.

In the class, I learned from contemporary essayist Phillip Lopate that the hallmark of the personal essay is its intimacy—its ability to embrace and question all that makes us who and why we are without ever professing to find the answer.[1] From Michel de Montaigne, I learned that essays are a way to observe the world from its "loftiest throne" while "sitting only on our own rump."[2] From Joan Didion, I learned that "life changes in the instant. The ordinary instant."[3] And from George Orwell and Gore Vidal, I learned that candor and confession are infinitely more powerful than perfection.

Unlike facts or statistics, personal stories are powerful not in spite of but because of their glaring subjectivity. Because real life is not heaven, essayists do not pretend to be angels. They toast with fervor such feelings as arrogance, despair, anger, guilt, and resentment. They address again and again what is viscerally painful. They judge their subjects honestly and approach life in all its undeniable reality, which in the end, reminds us that our subjects are always ourselves.

Thus, personal essayists tell stories to encapsulate the constant challenge of finding beauty even in life's most hideous moments. They tell the truth as they see it, which protects them from haughty overgeneralization. They find meaning and comfort in almost everything that flies their way, if only because they must. In doing so, essayists earn our empathy and, more importantly, our trust.

---

1   Phillip Lopate, "Introduction," in *The Art of the Personal Essay: An Anthology from the Classical Era to the Present*, ed. by Phillip Lopate (New York: Anchor Books, 1995), xxiii.

2   Michel de Montaigne, "On Experience," in *The Complete Essays*, ed. by M. A. Screech (New York: Penguin Press, 1993), 1207-1270.

3   Joan Didion, *The Year of Magical Thinking* (New York: Vintage Books, 2005), 3.

Beyond writing our own stories, we benefit tremendously from listening to them. In *Dad's Maybe Book*, a series of love letters to his sons, Tim O'Brien writes, "In great stories, as in life, we are confronted with raw presence. Events don't annotate themselves."[4] In other words, stories allow us—even invite us—to insert our own thoughts and experiences into the pages. A distant character's happiness becomes our own, as does their anxiety, grief, passion, and fear.

In my own essays, I want my stories to set the stage for someone else's scenes. I ask that my readers fill in the gaps with their own lines and props and characters. My life is not as significant as I sometimes make it out to be, but my feelings are universal—like love and the desire to control it, like loneliness in a listless crowd and the promise to leave it, like happiness and the hope that anxiety, depression, or any of their close cousins do not snatch it away.

These are all feelings that extend beyond me. These are stories that, regardless of author, make us feel a little less alone. For when we are by ourselves, stories are what keep us honest company. They ask us to confront a scene's raw presence and in doing so, confront ourselves. They articulate the truths of each moment as we continue to ask:

"Who am I? What do I want? And why?"

As young adults, our biggest truth is this: we are confronting life during perhaps its most contradictory period. We are accidental experts of naïvety and maturity, innocence and experience. We are also earnest beginners entering a tumultuous world—one we are poised to change in every possible way.

---

4   Tim O'Brien, *Dad's Maybe Book* (New York: Houghton Mifflin, 2019), 129.

Four years ago, I entered college excited and terrified for everything to come. Now, I am excited and terrified for everything that comes next. As a neurotic planner predisposed to organizing every filing cabinet of life, I work toward the future with calculating unease. This book is my first step toward acknowledging that planning for milestones is not nearly as cathartic as living the seemingly random sequence of events that carry me there. My essays, now and in the future, will document my attempts to make sense of it all, piece by piece.

In the introduction to his anthology *The Art of the Personal Essay,* Lopate writes that few personal essayists who have made names for themselves are young, much less twenty-one years young. Yet he also states that "to essay is to attempt, to test, to make a run at something without knowing whether you are going to succeed."[5] If writers truly succeed through trial by fire, through failure, and through a confusion of the self, then I will succeed at storytelling by experimenting with it.

With twenty-one years gone and, with good luck and good health, many more to go, I will tell my stories to make sense of the ones to come. I will stand in the midst of the passionate turbulence that is the hallmark of youth and reflect on it with the hallmark of the essay—intimacy.

At the time this book is published, most of our generation will be standing at the juncture where the roads of childhood end and those of adulthood begin. With many roads closed and many more to be taken, together we will forge into the labyrinth ahead.

---

5   Lopate, "Introduction," in *The Art of the Personal Essay,* xxiii-liv.

Along the way, we will listen to the stories of others and collect our own. We will tell them to keep ourselves going, and we will polish the meaningful truths they become under the sandpaper of time.

These will be the truths we hold dear as we grow up.

These will be the stories we pass down as we grow old.

SO IT GOES

———

After spending four months of my college years in Europe, I was ready to come home not as a bumbling nineteen-year-old but as an independent and responsible adult. On the flight back from Prague, I imagined my parents' look of surprise when they saw me, not in my usual Nike sweatpants and oversized hoodie, but in a violet button-down blouse, heather gray boots, and zippered fur overcoat I bought on Republic Square. Never mind that I made the purchase inside PALLA-DIUM, an ultra-modern shopping mall housing the likes of Calvin Klein, Lush, and H&M or that, save for a swift *děkuji* at the end, I conducted my entire transaction in English. All my parents had to know was that I had acquired a beautiful winter coat near Wenceslas Square and the Old Town of Prague. *Wow*, my dad would say to me in Mandarin. *You are so grown up now. My beautiful world traveler.*

I began selecting the stories I would tell my parents long before the flight home: How I had traveled to Slovenia alone and befriended an Italian connoisseur and a Singaporean journalist at the annual wine festival. How I had danced with Ralph Kiefer, a street pianist in Munich, and became penpals with him afterward. How I ended up driving to another country at 1 a.m. because the only thing my friends had wanted after getting wasted at the Delirium Cafe in Belgium were Spicy Taco Supremes from Taco Bell and weed, and the small town of Eindhoven, Netherlands, was the closest place where they could splurge on both.

As soon as the gate opened and the people in front of me had cleared out with their bags, I bolted out of the plane and flew toward baggage claim. Houston comforts swirled by in a colorful blur—tall cowboy hats and rhinestoned jeans, lighthearted hoots of "y'all" and "buhbye, sweetheart," the smoky aroma of brisket and baby back ribs at a Pappas Bar-B-Q joint stationed right next to the security checkpoint.

I was panting by the time I reached the area marked Baggage Claim A. I scanned the crowd for three familiar faces, but my older sister, Elaine, saw me first. I heard her call my name from behind me. Before I could turn to see her, I was knocked forward in an aggressive hug that felt like home.

"Welcome back!" she said.

"I missed you," I sniffed.

"God, you're still so sappy. Med school's been too busy for me to miss you." She laughed when I turned around with a pout. "Kidding! Just kidding." But when I started to laugh with her, she stopped. She looked me up and down slowly and began squeezing my arms.

"What are you doing, Eli?" I squirmed out of her grasp.

"Amy, did you lose a lot of weight while you were abroad?"

"What do you mean?"

"Nothing. You just look . . . never mind. Let's go get mom and dad."

We both turned to see them waving at us. They cocked their heads to one side when they saw my sister's face. *How could one of you be in a bad mood already?* they seemed to ask.

When I picked out the stories I wanted to tell my family during my semester in Prague, I purposely left out any that involved my anxiety, my attempts to starve myself, or my late-night phone calls with Elaine. I called her whenever I had confessions to make. I called to disclose uncomfortable, embarrassing, and disgusting things.

One time, I confessed I had eaten avocado toast for dinner and that, for hours after the meal, I alternated between throwing up chunks of compost-colored mush into the kitchen sink and swallowing it back down. I confessed I sometimes spit out my regurgitations into street trash cans and other times, when I couldn't hold it any longer, right onto the streets. I confessed I would rather spit stomach acid out than let it go back in.

Another time, I confessed that I hated my feet. I had always hated my feet—especially when I was an obese little kid who could never fit them into anything other than wide sneakers—but this time, I was confessing that some nights, I cried myself to sleep because no matter how many pairs of socks I wore, my feet always felt like they were encased in ice. I confessed I felt cold all the time. I confessed that feeling cold was starting to make me act cold, too.

Once, I called Elaine to confess I was scared of my own anger. My roommate Wes had hugged me around the waist earlier that day, and I had flinched and yelled at him not to touch me there because "that's where the fat rolls are." When he told me I wasn't fat, I yelled at him to stop lying. I never told him how secretly pleased I was that he thought 102 pounds was "too low," that I was "too skinny." Because growing up, I remember dreaming of the day someone would say that to me, genuinely.

I confessed to Elaine I felt guilty for yelling at him; I also confessed I felt thrilled. Wes had remembered I was "only" 102 pounds. It made me want to lose more, to prove I could control anything about myself if only I tried hard enough.

The next time I called Elaine was to report that another month had gone by without getting my period.

"Eli?"

"What's up?"

"My uterus has decided to cling to my insides for another month."

"What the heck, Amy. Gross."

"AKA I didn't get my period. I'm just trying to see if humor is my thing."

"It's not."

"Rude."

"How long has it been again since you had your last one?" I stared at the ceiling and counted the months in my head. I wondered whether or not I should lie.

"A little over two years now."

I heard static on the line, then a panicked whisper. "Amy, what?"

"It's okay, it's okay, Eli." This was a lie. "It's not like I'm not *trying* to get it back. It'll come back … someday. But right now, it's whatever, right? It's nice to not have cramps and deal with all the blood anyway. Also, think about all the money I've saved on pads and tampons."

"And what about throwing up and feeling cold all the time? Don't you think there's something else going on?"

"Maybe, I don't know. I promise I'm having the time of my life, I think. Just minus the exhaustion and the stress."

"That doesn't sound normal to me."

"You're just paranoid."

The following month, Elaine called me.

"Amy, did you get your period?"

"Nope."

"Okay. Actually, Amy, I think I know what's going on. But just to make sure before I say anything, I want you to talk to a professional. Can I make you an appointment for when you get home? Is that okay? Amy?"

"Okay," I whispered. No response. I tried again, a little more upbeat. "Yeah, that'd be great. I definitely want kids one day. So, you know, I can't be infertile forever."

"Ok, Amy, very funny—"

"Told you I was funny."

"Take care of yourself."

"I am."

I somehow convinced myself that, by the time I flew home, Elaine would have forgotten about those phone calls, just as conveniently as I left them out of my stories. I wanted people to see me as an invincible study abroad veteran so I could feel like one, too. Contacting a shoe store regarding my stolen wallet in Barcelona? No problem. Brushing my teeth in the basement wash closet of a Viennese hostel because I had a three-hour layover at a closed bus terminal? Check. Calling an ambulance after a delayed nut allergy attack left me gasping for air in the basement of an Albert supermarket? Sure, and I'll puncture my leg with my EpiPen needle while I wait. That's just what adults do.

I was once told that stories make for the best gifts. If so, I wanted to bring back only the good ones. Nothing depressing, nothing self-pitying, nothing that would take away the fact I was young, reckless, naïve, and deliriously happy to be all three. I could afford to wear rose-tinted glasses at the age of nineteen. What was wrong with being optimistic about immortality?

A stranger answered my question the following week when Elaine took me to see a place called, blandly, Wellness Coaching & Nutrition Therapy.

"I'm proud of you for agreeing to do this, Amy," Elaine said as she drove us down the highway. I wanted to strangle her for caring so much.

"Try not to be nervous," she went on. "Just talk to her like you did with me. She can tell us what's really going on."

"Can you stop being so serious, Eli? You're freaking me out. It's not like I'm dying or something." I saw her grip the wheel harder.

"Eli, why did you look so sad when you picked me up at the airport?"

"Because it felt like I was hugging a skeleton, Amy. A wrinkly sack of bones."

"Oh."

We parked in the garage of a mud-colored brick building. When we stepped inside, a pasty woman named Heather greeted us at the door. She wore plain brown flats and a frilled blouse that looked like it came from Loft, the chain store where I imagine old people shop to replicate "office chic." Her red hair looked slightly fried, as if someone had microwaved it before fanning it out in the humid Houston air.

I walked into her room, sat on the edge of a cold leather couch, and found myself surrounded by plastic plates and rubber, life-size molds of different foods: rubber broccoli, rubber white bread, rubber mac and cheese, rubber red roasted potatoes, rubber almonds, rubber pork chops, rubber chicken, rubber personal pizza, rubber brownie, rubber apple, and rubber kid's size milk carton.

What in the actual hell?

"So, Amy, I understand you're here to get your period back, correct?"

No shit, Sherlock. "Yes, ma'am."

"Okay. I'm going to ask you a few questions about your eating habits. Just answer them as honestly as you can, okay?"

"Yes, ma'am."

"Can you tell me about yourself and your relationship with food, both now and when you were growing up?"

I mentioned being addicted to diets. I mentioned growing up as the fat kid and how in my junior year of high school, when I finally hit 129 pounds, I promised myself I'd finally start losing weight, hard and fast. I mentioned exercising two hours a day and calorie-counting on MyFitnessPal. I mentioned counting the number of blueberries I ate for breakfast each morning and starving myself until I was in pain.

"Can you describe how your eating habits have changed from then until now? How does restricting the amount of food you eat and only eating 'healthy' things make you feel?"

I told her I felt superior to other people when I ate less than they did. I told her I liked seeing the gap between my thighs grow and the number on the scale shrink.

"While you were in Europe, what would a typical lunch look like?"

"Two cups of broccoli, carrots, and shredded ham."

"Mhm. And how about dinner?"

"Half an avocado, grilled chicken, salad, no dressing."

"Mhm. And how many carbs would you say you eat a day?"

No answer.

"Can you portion out a full day's carbs for me?" she repeated, her gaze turning toward the rubber foods.

I gestured to a one-inch thick piece of flabby sponge bread. "Half of that, maybe."

"And how many vegetables?"

I picked up rubber green beans, rubber carrots, and the rubber broccoli bunch, which I began to use as a stress ball.

"I see. And what do you think a *normal* person would likely eat in a day?"

"Excuse me?"

"Well, a *normal* meal usually consists of two servings of carbohydrates"—she picked up the rubber bread and the rubber potatoes—"one serving of vegetables"—the rubber broccoli took flight—"three servings of protein"—then came three rubber pork chops—"and one serving of fat." She picked up some rubber cheese cubes. "You don't seem to be eating all of this in any single meal," she said softly.

After asking a couple more questions that implied something was wrong with me, Heather sighed, folded her hands, and nodded sympathetically. I wanted to take the rubber steak off her plate and smack the quizzical expression off her face. But before I could gather the courage to go through with it, she began speaking again.

"Well, the good news is we can definitely help you get your period back. It's not uncommon for our patients to experience menstruation irregularities."

Who said I was going to be your patient? "That's so ... relieving to hear."

"Well, yes, but I'm afraid I'll have to refer you to someone else to begin the actual treatment process."

"I'm sorry, I don't understand."

Elaine chimed in. "Heather, can you elaborate a bit? What is Amy dealing with? And who should she see?"

"Well, from what I'm hearing—Amy, correct me if I'm wrong—she seems to be struggling with orthorexia, which is a kind of eating disorder that focuses on obsessive healthy eating, weight loss, and compulsive exercising. It often transforms into more serious eating disorders, which Amy seems to exhibit many symptoms of, like feeling cold and anxious." She turned to me again.

"Amy, I think what you have is something called 'anorexia nervosa.' It's more commonly known as anorexia. Does that sound familiar at all?" I pictured the girls whose bodies looked like skeletons to be hung up for Halloween.

"Yes," I squeaked, "but no one's ever called me anorexic before. It sounds a bit extreme."

"I think you should get some lab tests done—just to be safe. I'll be referring you to a physician who can give you a more well-informed diagnosis."

As soon as we left her office, I turned to Elaine and asked, "I don't actually have to do this, right?"

"I think you should," she said. "For the record, Amy, I think Heather is right. After what you told me on our phone calls, I thought you had an eating disorder, too. I was afraid to be right, which is why I wanted you to see someone else first."

"Oh." For some reason, I felt ashamed. Guilty. "So what does that mean?"

"I guess we'll find out next week."

On Monday, I found myself in another office. "Every body is beautiful," said a plaque in the seating area. That sign—along with two glowing lamps, blue-cloth sofas with matching pillows and navy blankets, and the dark chestnut floors—felt forced. The environment was designed to calm me down, which only made me sweat more. A tall woman with aggressively blue eyes and an intimidating smile asked me to come in and lie on her medical exam table.

"Hi Amy, I'm Jennifer. How are you feeling today?" she asked as she took my blood pressure.

"Fine. Great." I smiled, my heart beating fast.

"Do you know why you're here today?"

"My nutritionist referred me."

"Yes, I spoke with Heather over the phone. I'm glad you're here. Any dizziness?" she asked as she took my pulse lying down, then standing up.

"No."

"Your fingers are cold."

"Sorry."

"Your skin also looks a little orange."

"I think I ate too many carrots while I was in Europe," I squeaked.

"Interesting. And how many carrots did you typically eat every day?"

She had to be joking.

"Um," I cleared my throat. "Maybe two or three big ones. They're really crunchy. And healthy. Sometimes I'd share with my friends."

"Okay, do me a favor and stop eating carrots for a bit." She placed her hands around my throat and started massaging the skin over my thyroid, as if she were pressing keys on a piano.

Yep, this lady is officially crazy.

"Your skin looks orange because you've been eating too much beta-carotene found in orange vegetables. I heard you like vegetables—much more than fats and carbs, I'm guessing?" I swallowed. Jennifer told me to lie back down again. She walked over to where my sister was sitting and whispered something to her. Elaine nodded. Her face was pale.

Jennifer walked back to me and began pressing into my stomach.

"Honey, I don't want to shock you. But I want you to know your sister saved your life by making that appointment." I blinked at her.

"You're severely malnourished, honey. Your thyroid has shrunk, your immune system is down, and your hands and feet feel so cold all the time because your body no longer has the energy to circulate blood normally to the extremities."

"Oh." Now, I felt dizzy.

"It took me a while to find your pulse because it was weak," she continued. "Thirty-nine beats per minute—do you have any idea what that means?"

I saw Elaine put her hand to her mouth. I shook my head.

"A normal heart rate is about sixty to eighty beats per minute. Maybe, *maybe* if you were a marathon runner or an Olympic athlete, it'd be closer to fifty. But for any normal person, sixty beats is the minimum. Anything under fifty gets you sent straight to the emergency room. You've lost twenty-seven pounds since your junior year of high school, correct? The fact that you just spent the past four months running around Europe is crazy. It is, quite literally, unbelievable."

I stared at her, and I must have looked crazy, too, because she stopped talking for a second and cradled me up into a sitting position. In a softer, slower voice, she said, "Sweetie, I'm surprised you managed to convince everyone around you, including your parents, that you were doing okay. You should have had a heart attack by now."

No. I shook my head slowly. She was wrong. I didn't believe her. She was lying. I looked at Elaine. *Tell me she's lying*, I wanted to ask. But I didn't need to; I could tell by Elaine's expression what her answer would have been. I shut my eyes. The tears came anyway. Jennifer asked me to schedule my follow-up appointment. She told me one last thing before I left for the front desk.

"Amy, you're lucky to be alive."

In one afternoon, I went from being an empowered young adult taking on the world to a self-destructive patient fighting to stay alive. The next time I saw Jennifer, my whole family came with me. Jennifer talked about meal plans and treatment programs. I opted for outpatient therapy because a ten-week hospital stay would never let me be a normal college kid again.

But Jennifer read my mind. As soon as I told her I didn't want to do an inpatient program—on the basis of financial cost and inconvenience and "that kind of thing"—she advised my parents not to let me return to NYU that spring.

"It's just not safe for her to go back. Even if she chooses outpatient treatment, she can't battle her eating disorder voice remotely. Or alone."

I knew Jennifer had lost. My hardworking immigrant parents, who had always frowned upon skipping school even for illness, would never let me skip an entire semester of college. My education was their paramount necessity—a nonnegotiable. I waited for them to tell Jennifer my flight had already been purchased and my classes already arranged.

Instead, my dad told me Jennifer was right. "Let's keep you here, Amy. We . . . we had no idea things were this bad."

"No dad, I'll be fine. I'm *fine*."

"That's what you always said on the phone. We—" his voice broke. "Your mom and I can't trust you to take care of yourself right now. When we go home, I'm canceling your flight back to New York. I'm sorry."

"But dad—"

"No buts."

"But you always say education is the most important thing!"

"Is it more important than your life?"

"Mom—"

"You're not going back, Amy."

I remember running out of the room after that. I remember running away from Jennifer, away from my parents who had betrayed me, away from my diagnosis and the truth. I remember locking myself in the stall of the women's bathroom, crying until my face broke out in rashes from all the tissue paper I had used to scrub away the snot. I remember crying all the way home and crying myself to sleep later that night, too. I do not remember much else.

In a surreal collapsing of time, the second semester of my sophomore year came and went without me. Instead of going back to school, I stayed in Houston, where my insecurities were laid out to dry under the blistering Texas sun. My days consisted of visits to my therapist's high-rise office in River Oaks, where I spent more time looking at the downtown skyline than at her. My nights consisted of silent family meals and evening walks with my parents. The cicadas sang and the toads croaked and I said nothing, listening to my parents tell me that everything would be okay.

Scattered between these moments were the hours I spent alone with my books. I read David Sedaris, Kurt Vonnegut, Viet Thanh Nguyen, David Foster Wallace, Tim O'Brien, J.D. Salinger, Zora Neale Hurston, Jhumpa Lahiri, and Atul Gawande. I immersed myself in their worlds to forget my own. I came to realize books were better therapists than any hour-long session two hundred dollars could buy because, with books, there were no forced conversations, no expectations, no unwanted transactions. There were simply characters and the actions they took and the events that transpired, from which I could take away anything I pleased.

On a day when I was filled with particular self-loathing, I read Kurt Vonnegut's *Slaughterhouse Five* and fell in love with the ubiquitous phrase: "So it goes." It was a statement the narrator said whenever he found himself grappling with fatalism, death, or trauma—any kind of event out of his control. "So it goes."[6]

And so my days went. When I realized there was nothing else I could do, I began the first of many attempts to accept my new reality.

In February, I signed myself up for singing lessons at Vivaldi Music School. In March, after I'd gained enough weight, I started taking dance classes at Soundbox Studios. When the weather turned nice, I began taking solo strolls around the neighborhood, belting the words to "Heaven" by Bryan Adams while strumming my ukulele. In April, I started eating more and caring less. I began feeling better about my body, which meant I sometimes went for days at a time

---

6   Kurt Vonnegut, *Slaughterhouse-Five* (New York: Dial Press, 2009).

without thinking about it at all. I stopped calling myself a failure. I genuinely felt lucky for my second chance at life. I lived David Foster Wallace's clichés boldly and unironically and Hung In There.

Of course, there were still days when I cried at myself in the mirror and left red claw marks on my stomach. There were also days where I described myself as a "fat whale" in my journal, but those days became less and less frequent. "So it goes," I would write after another episode of tears. The words became a ritualistic shield against my own inner demons.

By the time May rolled around, I was twenty pounds heavier. But what I had put on in physical pounds, I seemed to have shed in mental weight. I woke up one morning wanting to eat a glazed chocolate donut; I went out and bought it. I woke up the next morning not wanting to exercise, so I did not. It felt stupid to say, even to think, but it was not long before I was waking up dreaming of an endlessly optimistic future again.

At the end of the month, Jennifer cleared me for my return. She seemed convinced that this time, when I promised my family I would take care of myself, I meant it. I packed my bags for New York City. I was eager to see my friends, and I was ready to allow myself to be seen.

On my first stroll through lower Manhattan since last August, New York looked exactly as I had left it. Aside from a few restaurants on St. Mark's that had closed and reopened as ramen shops and the new deli on 8th Street, the rest of it was all there: the Strand Book Store on Broadway with its one- to five-dollar book trolleys, the honking cars never where they needed to be, the sandaled couples in Washington Square Park with their dogs and their Irving Farm iced coffees, and the NYU summer students walking from

Bobst Library to the Starbucks on 4th Street for a friendlier place to study.

With Franz Kafka's *The Metamorphosis* in tow, I sat down on a wooden bench in Washington Square Park and watched a group of friends, an elderly couple, and a family of four pass under the Washington Arch. While I had been home, these people had been dutifully living their lives. None of them knew me, nor did they know I had been here exactly a year ago, sitting on this same bench, taking summer in New York City for granted. I guess no one really cared.

Even so, I took comfort in being there with them in the park, listening to an amateur jazz ensemble play The Beatles covers by the fountain. Despite the fact that they were out of tune and a little too loud, I felt moved just to be able to sit there and listen, to soak in the improvised notes and the syncopated snares.

I eased back further into my bench and held the book in my lap. I was waiting for a friend to come and read until sunset with me. Perhaps he would notice the tears in my eyes as we sat there listening to a guitarist, a bassist, a trumpet player, and a percussionist jam away to "Here Comes the Sun" on an ordinary summer afternoon.

HOW TO GET YOUR MONEY STOLEN AND HOW TO DEAL WITH ALL YOUR EMOTIONS AFTERWARD

———

During my semester abroad in Prague in 2017, I called my mom and sister one night, snot-nosed and teary-eyed, to tell them that all the money I kept stashed in my drawers had been stolen. Those 27,000 korunas—about $1,150 worth of cold, hard, pastel-colored cash—were supposed to last me the rest of my time in Europe. When I discovered it was all gone, I did what any sane person would do in my situation: crawl into bed and wail like a cow.

I composed myself enough to call home an hour later. As I dialed my mom's cell, I played out our conversation in my head: there would be my sob story, then a much-deserved scolding, and finally the reassuring statement that in the end, everything would be okay. Instead, my sob story was met with spastic laughter over the line. The scolding consisted of my mom telling me to buck up and get over myself. My sister, who was with her at the time, chimed in and suggested that rather than cry about my financial trauma, I should "write about it instead."

"It would be so much funnier than what you usually write."

I cried harder after that.

The next morning, I woke up with swollen eyes and a nasty headache, but I felt slightly better knowing my mom hadn't wanted to kill me for hiding money in "the most obvious place possible" and then losing it. I was also slightly relieved to realize I was not a complete idiot: while the cash in the drawer was all gone, the debit card I kept inside my underwear was still there. I could use that to draw out some emergency cash. I called my mom again to tell her my plan, and then I promised to pay her back with "lots and lots of interest, after I get a job one day."

I took a walk down Machova Street to withdraw a few thousand Czech korunas at the corner ATM. When I came back, I hid the crisp bills everywhere: in my coat pockets, in between laundry sheets, in the fabric folds of padded bras, underneath my Danish butter cookie bin—everywhere except my drawers. Once I was satisfied with my work, I sat down at my desk and proceeded to bang out a blog post "much funnier" than my past travel posts.

As I wrote, I grudgingly acknowledged that my sister was right—I do tend to write better when I am angry or bitter or depressed or, better yet, all three. In fact, the more pissed off I get, the faster and more engaging the writing becomes. This seems to be the case for many writers who have produced fabulous work in an agitated state of mind (think David Foster Wallace in his rant about the horrors of cruise ships, David Sedaris in his stint as a Macy's elf, or Jamaica Kincaid in her tirade on the clusterfuck politics and frigid materialism of Miami Beach). As I wrote, I also thought back to what Mrs. Weissenstein had once told me in a high school creative writing class: "Perfect days make for terrible stories, and vice versa." I kept that in mind as I spent the rest of that weekend holed up in my dorm room, writing the perfect story about a shitty day.

I published the piece the following week as a cheeky, self-deprecating blog post. I started it off with a grainy photograph of Leonardo DiCaprio tossing away wads of cash from a yacht, which had been superimposed with self-pitying white letters: "YOU CAN'T SAVE MONEY YOU DON'T HAVE." After I wrote the post, I decided it was not irreverent enough, so I went back and did "control, find, replace" for every mention of the word "money" with "**cash money $$$**" to spice up the prose. I later submitted that original post to my editor, but she told me to "highly consider rewriting the whole thing" for a book that, presumably, would show the maturation of my thoughts as I grew up.

So I rewrote the whole thing and changed every "**cash money $$$**" back to simply "cash" or "money." I was sad to see the "**$$$**"s go, but I suppose not much meaning was truly lost. The essay is still a satirical, irreverent, and petty attack on the crooks who stole from me. It still expresses my hope that if they one day find this book and read it (highly unlikely), they will feel my curdled wrath. And it still describes, with great fervor and historical accuracy, the (personal) financial crisis I endured in the fall of 2017 and all the life lessons I learned along the way as I, a nineteen-year-old child, gallivanted across Europe.

I lost my first wad of cash in Barcelona, the city known for beaches and *chiringuitos*, Gaudi's colorful mosaics and free-flowing buildings, *discotecas* and attractive *futbolistas*, and, of course, petty pickpockets.

Over fall break, my friends and I happened to be in Barcelona to enjoy all these things. We also happened to be there on the warm September evening of La Mercè, Barcelona's annual festival in which locals celebrate Catalan traditions and religious folklore through peculiar activities such as the *correfoc*, a "fire-run" in which fire-wielding "devils" run through the streets in an attempt to burn innocent members of the public; *la sardana*, a hand-holding dance that is preceded and followed by wriggling human pyramids; and the *ball de gegants*, a "ball of the giants" in which two-story papier-mâché figures that look like everything from a biblical shepherd to Lord Farquaad from *Shrek* are paraded through the city with music.

Because this festival is planned by locals, my friends and I ended up among the confused tourists who, upon seeing what we thought were giant Barbie dolls dressed for either marriage, war, or serfdom, got swept into the roaring crowds.

From the center of the mob, we caught brief glimpses of people in black capes and horned devil masks running down the streets, wielding sparklers and firebrands the size of yard sticks. A golden metallic dragon sat on its haunches in the back lines, spraying sparklers at stragglers. And, a few blocks away, giant papier-mâché heads bobbed along to the sound of trumpets and drums.

As for us, we jogged along with *jóvenes* who looked far too happy to be running from fire. I felt like I was participating in a Pamplona bull run, except the bulls were humans. Yet, partly because I was curious and partly because the streets were too crowded to leave, I stumbled along and cheered with everyone else.

I held tight to my tote bag as I enjoyed the literal cultural immersion. While Tripadvisor had failed to introduce me to the most celebrated festival in the city, it had done an exceedingly good job in warning me about its pickpockets. As soon as I felt the crowd closing in on me, I moved my bag to the front and, for extra measure, kept my left hand in the front pocket the entire time to prevent anyone else from poking around.

But I must have taken my hand out at one point or another—perhaps to pump my fists during the fire runs or to cover my ears during the explosive fireworks—I do not really remember. All I remember was later that evening, when I ran into the nearest convenience store in search of some emergency tampons, I realized my wallet was no longer in my bag.

I screamed bloody murder right there in the store.

My friend Jesse found me somehow. I asked him to buy me a box of tampons. He apologized to a terrified cashier as he did so. Outside, he asked me what in the world was going on. In between colorful expletives and snotty gasps, I informed him that my wallet, which—mind him—carried my dorm keys, my driver's license, my credit card, and all 400 euros I had just withdrawn from the ATM outside La Boqueria earlier that day, had gone missing in the parade.

I sulked all evening while my friends got sangria-wasted by the beach. I sulked for the remainder of my time in Spain, too.

Two mornings later, we were in Madrid having brunch at a cute little spot called Ojalá. To cut my losses, I refused to order food. When the entrées came for everyone else—dulce de leche and jam tostadas, *jamón ibérico* eggs benedict, grated tomato and olive oil toast, ricotta with tapenade, and "Bonbon" coffee with condensed milk and a shot of Bailey's—I stood up, excused myself from the table, and ran down San Andrés Street, spending the next hour trying to get lost in the neighborhood of Malasaña. Jesse found me, again. This time, I was in a Carrefour, sniffling and mindlessly squeezing the lumpy green pears in the produce section.

"I'm hungry," I mumbled when I saw the expression on his face.

"Do you want something?"

"No. I mean, yes. But only if you can make my wallet magically appear again."

My wallet reappeared on the night we left Spain. On the drive to Madrid–Barajas Airport, I received an e-mail from a shoe store in the Gothic Quarter of Barcelona saying that a salesclerk had found a maroon wallet underneath a used shoe rack, and that they had found this email address on a slip of paper inside. The sender specified that some keys, a Texas driver's license, and a (cancelled) credit card were still inside.

There was no way for me to turn back and get it, but there was one other group of NYU Prague students who would be there for one more night. I texted them and begged someone to retrieve it for me.

"I'll pay you back in Prague. I still have cash there. Umm ... *por favor*."

When a girl named Shinyi texted back saying she had picked it up, I went from being the unluckiest girl in the world to the luckiest. 400 lost euros no longer seemed so bad—at least I could get back into my room in Prague and bathe myself in Czech korunas.

A month passed before the fateful morning of October 25, 2017 came around, and I went right back to being the most pissed off, unlucky sonofabitch again. I had opened my drawers to pull out some more cash (I had run out buying too many carrots at Albert Supermarket) only to find out the 27,000 korunas I (rather idiotically) kept stored there had disappeared. Gone. Stolen. Poof!

My initial thought was one of extreme déjà vu. It was Barcelona all over again. Except this time it was much, much worse.

That was when I called my mom and sister.

The blog post came right after, as did the two lists of "life lessons" I discussed afterwards, filled with wonderful advice on how to act as the innocent victim of money theft.

PART 1 OF *AMY'S GUIDE TO GETTING YOUR MONEY STOLEN*: DIDDLY SQUAT COMMON SENSE

1. When traveling, make sure you always carry a nice purse with you in the most crowded, touristy part of town. Give someone the opportunity to take advantage of you, or as locals in Colombia say, "Give papaya."

2. Make sure you're squeezed against as many strangers as possible so they can, at any second, unzip your purse and snatch away your cute maroon wallet like the ripe little papaya it is.

3. Don't check your purse for suspicious activity until you need it to buy tampons at a random convenience store.

4. Realize your wallet is gone and say "oh my God" one hundred times fast because you know this is the foolproof way to get God Himself to appear and deliver not one, but *two* new wallets to you, pronto.

5. Cry a lot when God doesn't show up.
6. Tell yourself you'll make up for the loss by not spending any more cash. Because starving yourself of future food and fun is the only way to regain happiness.
7. Attempt to place blame on someone and then ultimately blame yourself.
8. Feel guilty.
9. Continue to feel guilty and cry about it every night in the Airbnb.
10. Make everyone around you feel awkward because they're all lying in bunk beds next to you.

P.S. While you're out traveling, make sure to leave excess cash in an obvious place in the room. Make sure it's practically out in the open and that it's all in one spot, too. Don't bother wasting the precious minute it takes to hide the cash in different places around the room—this makes you that paranoid jerk who has no chill.

PART 2 OF *AMY'S GUIDE TO GETTING YOUR MONEY STOLEN*: JOIN THE DRAMA CLUB

Now that you've lost all your cash not once, but *twice*, because you have diddly squat common sense, there are a few things you need to do.

1. Feel intense pity for yourself. You just lost wads of cash, and your life sucks, and no one else has it worse than you.
2. Pull out more cash, but don't put it all in the same place again because you are, in fact, an average individual with common sense.

3. Continue hating on the person who stole your original cash by imagining how many Czech potatoes he/she could be buying with it (well over 3,500—and now imagine if those were *your* potatoes).

4. Back up for a second and think, *So many people have it worse than I do, and therefore I am a terrible person for thinking "x" in the first place.*

5. Keep repeating steps 1, 3, and 4 until you are mentally and physically exhausted and your eyes are legitimate cocoa puffs.

6. Pass out in bed at 4 a.m. and stay passed out until your suitemate knocks on your door to tell you class is in ten minutes.

7. Curse his ability to make you feel guilty about missing class and sprint out the door, your eyes still looking like those cocoa puffs.

After the blog post came out, the rest of the semester passed by as any other semester abroad usually would: with cheap Pilsner and Staropramen towers and boxed wine, late-night clubbing before presentations and exams, and trips each weekend to a new country where, in between museum visits and city tours, I would always make my way to tourist trap zones to buy three postcards—one for myself, one for my family, and one for my boyfriend.

All those days blended together in a sweet, nostalgic sort of way, the way Neapolitan ice cream does when the vanilla, chocolate, and strawberry stripes melt into one thick syrup. Each additional day in Europe made this syrup one degree thicker, one hint sweeter.

While the majority of my time was either spent in my dorm room, in class, or on a bus, train, or plane, a few exceptional moments stand out like glistening cherries on top: watching the sun dip below the Mediterranean from the Cinque Terre cliffside with Jesse, climbing Petřín Hill with my childhood friend Amber, biking along the canals of Amsterdam with John, stuffing myself with La Mallorquina pastries in Madrid, or stepping on all the autumn leaves in Munich's Englishgarten, convinced they were the richest coppers and yellows and wine reds I had ever seen.

Funnily enough, the robberies also became some of those cherries on top, albeit sour ones. The horrible moments of the trip became memorable for their absurdity and, in that way, defined it too—not that any NYU ambassador ever put it that way. I still remember how all the study abroad liaisons had told me with plastered smiles on their faces that "studying abroad changes your life!!!" It was the worst of clichés, but they convinced me to sign up anyway.

Looking back on that semester in Europe, I would say I learned the ordinary lessons of study abroad: how to navigate a foreign city, how to deal with people calling me "Ching Chong China Konichiwa!" (???), and how to travel light. But more important were the lessons in the extraordinary. In Slovenia, for instance, I discovered how to charm a five-star hotel's concierge into letting me take a much-needed shit in the lounge bathroom before a nine-hour overnight bus ride. In Prague, I enjoyed the rare experience of waking up naked in an unfamiliar hospital bed, hooked to nasal oxygen tubes and IV pumps after an episode of anaphylactic shock. I had not planned for these—the bathroom emergencies, the nut allergy attacks, the thefts—but for better or worse, the least expected moments were the ones that defined my trip.

Rereading my blog post, I realized my teacher Mrs. Weissenstein was right. Perfect days make for shitty stories because there is no suspense, no climax, no character development. I left Europe with a deep sense of appreciation and tenderness but also with the sentiment that a "perfect study abroad experience" is bullshit. In the real world, no safe spaces exist.

Two months after writing my blog post, I was robbed for the third and final time.

Caitlyn, my friend who was studying abroad in Florence that semester, decided we should celebrate the end of finals by traveling together. She met me in Prague, spent the weekend, and then together, we took the overnight train to Budapest as a last hurrah. On the ride there, we were dozing off in a small berth when a young European backpacker came in a little past midnight, sat down next to me, and started chatting with us in broken English. At some point, I stopped listening to him and fell back asleep. Before I knocked out, I pushed my wallet to the very bottom of my backpack and wrapped my hands instinctively around the straps. Of course, when I woke up, the backpacker was gone, as was my wallet.

No crying or screaming occurred. No phone call was placed to my mom. I was not flustered—I had already been through too much shit *not* to prepare for this, with all my cash stuffed in either my bra or my toiletry bag and only coins in my wallet. When I announced to Caitlyn that my wallet was gone again, that my debit card had been left in a Danish cookie box in Prague, and that I would pay her back for all expenses plus interest once I got back to the United States, she interrupted to ask if I was okay.

"Someone just stole your *wallet*, Amy! Are you sure you don't want to do something about it?"

"Very sure."

"Are you sure you're sure?"

"Yep. I was lucky enough to get it back the first time."

"You lost it once before?"

"Some guy in Barcelona ran off with it to get himself some used shoes."

"What?"

"It's all good. This new guy won't even be able to afford laces." The train pulled to a stop at Keleti Station. "Well, that's that," I said as we stepped onto Platform 12. "I'll get a job and pay you and my mom back when I get home. But for now, let's just have fun. We have three days to explore all of Budapest."

"You're handling this strangely well... but okay, deal. We need to try unicum at some point. It's a Hungarian national drink, and it's like 40 percent alcohol. Apparently it helps with digestion."

"Yes. Down. There's no way that's legal back home."

HE MEANS WELL

———

My dad tells me writing is a critical life skill. He says good writing will get me far (in what direction, I am not sure); he also says it will not get me far enough to make a living out of it. My dad says this about many "frivolous" things that I think would make for a good living—like teaching high school English, or becoming a travel journalist, or writing essays that explore what it actually means to "make a living." (But then again, I cannot expect him to understand when, to him, a substantial qualification for making a good living lies in the salary figure that supports it, because that was how he made his life in America possible—and mine too.)

My dad thinks I am brilliant. The trophies he has collected in his study room are his proof: golden figurines from Chinatown ping pong tournaments; music note medallions from Suzuki violin competitions; red and blue ribbons from Houston Rodeo Art; Olympic-sized medals from Scholastic Writing; a statue of a golden pheasant from the Tenth World Chinese Youth Talent Competition and a slim ballerina figurine from the Fourth Hong Kong International Dance Competition; an Honorable Mention plaque from the American Chemical Society; a gold-plated triangle from MATHCOUNTS; Junior Classical League ribbons for "outstanding achievement" in Latin; signed certificates from Toastmasters International, Girls Who Invest, Junior Achievement, and Kumon; my induction letter into Beta Gamma Sigma, the business school equivalent of Phi Beta Kappa; and the award I received for graduating as valedictorian of my NYU class. (Of course, graduating with a 4.0 GPA is nothing more than an extraordinarily embarrassing reminder that I have an anal knack for rule-following. Yet this is my dad's crown jewel, even though no one else would care.)

"Nǐ kàn kàn," he says. *Look at this.* He gestures to the trophy shelf once in a while, tells me it is proof of my potential, and, because I have potential, I have the unmistakable responsibility to live up to it.

"I grew up in a poor village in Henan, but I ended up attending the best university in all of China on scholarship," my dad reminds me every so often at the dinner table. "I had to work so hard for that opportunity. And I had to work hard after that, when I moved to America with almost no money. I got a master's degree at Lamar and worked night shifts at a fried chicken buffet just to pay the utility bills. Years later, after your mom came and we had settled down in Houston, we started this small homebuilder services company together. But it's nothing, really. It sounds like the dream but it's nothing. All we do now is kiss white people ass every day, even on weekends, all for what? For what? Don't be like me, Amy," he cautions. It would be *làngfèi*, a waste, to use all of my intelligence and ambition and hard work only to become a humble wordsmith—a "serious lack of judgment," he says in Mandarin with his sharp furrowed brows and his sour frown. "Anyone can write. Why not do something no one else can?"

Then he lists off the professions I should consider: CPA, asset manager, CEO, lawyer. If none of those work out, then maybe, *maybe*, as a last resort, a teacher—but only at the university level, and only if the administration offers tenure and favorable retirement benefits.

"Or just go be president. Imagine: Amy Dong, president of United States of America." He gestures at an imaginary banner in the sky and chuckles. He is only half joking.

But in the end, he always throws up his hands, sighs, and says, "Méi bàn fǎ." *I have no solution.* "Nǐ ài gànshénme jiù gànshénme." *Do what you want.* "You always look upset when I tell you how I feel. I am just telling you the truth, my experience, okay? I want you to be successful, be happy, be more than me." My dad tells me it was never his intention to stop me from dreaming. "Keep dreaming," he says. "Go be a writer," he says, "if that's what you really want. Go be naïve—I can't stop you."

So here I am, feeling horribly relieved and painfully guilty to be doing what I want, which is to write this damned book. Damned because every sentence is putting more distance between the person I am and the person he wants me to be. I spent all of college trying to be both and failed. Two summers on Wall Street only convinced me that shoulder-padded suits, old white bankers, and Excel spreadsheets were a special kind of hell. My financial accounting class felt like plucking my armpit hairs with tweezers—satisfying because there was always an end. I left business school still thinking I might go into law, but for reasons other than helping rich families get richer through corporate tax loopholes. I considered running for president at one point, but then 2016 happened, and if a white woman couldn't win against the biggest buffoon of the century, then who was I to think a Chinese woman could.

I am scared to tell my dad that I write not to entertain his dreams but to confess how much I hate them. I am scared to tell him most things, in fact, because I do not want to hurt him. He is someone who, despite his best efforts to hide them, has many feelings that cling to him tightly, seriously, anxiously. And because my dad loves with a selfish love, a tough love, a love boiling over with expectations for those he cares for most, I do not want to be the loved one who blows it all up.

Yet as long as my dad tells me to chase my dreams, I will continue to write. I will continue to tell stories, both to make a living and to make him proud. I will continue to dream, even if these dreams are not his.

Three memories of my father stand out above the rest.

I am twelve years old, and I have just won my first Silver Key for a painting I submitted to the Scholastic Art & Writing competition. It is a self-portrait in which I am sitting inside a hollow metal sculpture at Hermann Park, its copper beams wrapping themselves around me like a broken cage scintillating under the heat of the summer sun. I am looking up at its orange-white rays, and my back is toward the viewer so the light remains the central focus. I am alone but without an expression of loneliness, sitting there as if I have all the time in the world, inviting the viewer to daydream with me. The day I receive my award, I come home carrying the painting in my hands and the good news in my smile. My chest is puffed as I announce my achievement to my parents.

"I got a Silver Key for my painting!"

My mom smiles, my dad laughs, and I am about to run into his arms when he says to me, "Amy, your sister won a Gold Key her first year."

"Oh," I manage, my voice breaking a little.

"Come on, Amy, that was supposed to be a joke." I step away from him and run from the living room, looking up at the off-white ceiling to hold warm tears in place. I hear my mom yelling at him. I hear my dad defending himself because "Elaine really did win a Gold Key her first year," then my dad attempting to apologize, telling me this was just his type of humor. I think about the painting, about the fact that my sister had helped me title it "Enlightenment," and about how now, thanks to my dad, I feel everything but enlightened.

I am fourteen, and I am doing homework in the study when my mom comes in, squeezes my shoulder with her hand, and whispers in Mandarin, "Dad's father just passed away. He doesn't know I told you; don't make a scene."

I open the door and find my dad sitting at the dinner table, slouched in front of the lazy Susan with nothing in front of him and the lights off. He is alone. The secondhand of the clock ticks by sharply and infinitely, but his world is still. His glasses, which he only takes off before bed, now rest beside him on the table. He is staring straight ahead, his hands in his lap. The only things that move are the tears rolling down in silent, serious lines from his chin. I do not know if I should tell him I am here, or that I know what happened, or that I know everything will be okay, or the truth—that nothing is—so I just stand there, alone with him, watching. And soon I am crying too, not because I will never see my grandfather again, or because I will miss him, but because it is the first time I have ever seen my dad cry, and I am too shocked to do anything but cry with him. When he finally sees me, he stands up slowly, elegantly, like a swan lifting its head from calm waters, and makes a dignified turn into the hallway. His footsteps echo softly against the wooden floorboards until the delicate creak of his bed signals goodnight. We do not ever talk of this night again.

But for the next month, my dad drifts like a ghost, in and out of the past.

One night, he begins to reminisce about our last visit to his childhood home in the mountainous countryside of southeast China. It is a place where people weave bamboo baskets along dirt roads, where families live in *yaodongs,* homes carved from stone caves, and where his father lies buried, beneath the three-foot reeds overlooking a rocky cliffside.

"Remember when we all rode into town in your uncle's police car, and the sirens blared and scared all the chickens away? Remember how excited your grandma was to see us, and how much pleased she looked when we unloaded three whole suitcases of those duty-free Marlboro cigarettes she asked us to buy for her friends?" He laughs one throaty laugh. "But shit, what I really should have done is just given them all red envelopes of cash. If your grandpa hadn't been such a heavy smoker, he might have lived longer."

"But dad, you did give everyone cash. We had to go to the bank multiple times because you wanted them to have the new $100 bills. You're a hero to them. They all think you made it, you know. Lived the American Dream. I do, too. And so do Grandma and Grandpa."

"The American Dream, huh?" he snorts. "What kind of dream forces you to leave behind your own family?"

I am twenty-one years old, we have moved to a two-story house in Bellaire, and I am sitting at a new dinner table during a visit home from college. This time, the lazy Susan is not empty, but wobbling under heavy, home-cooked dishes that my parents and I have made together: tomato and scrambled egg, homegrown chives with minced garlic and olive oil, sweet potato and yellow millet soup, boiled peanuts and cold braised pig's feet. It is just the three of us. It almost feels like high school again, except now I am four years older, a little more in love with the world, and a little more skeptical of it, too. College has mellowed me out and taught me a lot—that saying no is harder than saying yes, that books teach more than classes do, and that traveling reminds me I am less important than I think I am. But mostly, college has taught me to treasure mundane things before they become rare, which is probably why I missed family meals more than I liked to admit. My dad seems to find family time more precious now, too, and more urgent, because in the middle of his next bite, he sets his chopsticks down on his bowl, clears his throat, and says, "Amy, now that you're a little older, I have something serious to talk to you about."

My mom looks at me and makes a face, but he ignores her and plows ahead.

"You've always been good with people, Amy. Always so many friends. You're smart, smarter than anyone else around you. And now you're almost done with college. You're about to start real life, you have so many options, so many people to help you, and I just want you to make sure you are making the right choices." He speaks loudly and breathlessly, stumbling over his words in a mix of Chinese and English as he rattles off thoughts he has been brewing for decades.

Perhaps he worries my mom or I will cut him off—it would not be the first time.

But unlike in high school, I do not interrupt or tell him to stop. His running start turns into a spiraling, hour-long monologue, in which he tells me he wants the world for me. The literal world, he means: money, a good title, my own home or several, just in case, and most of all, a family and everything I need to support it because everything he has done, he has done for family, and look how we turned out.

He starts talking about CPAs and CEOs and lawyers again. I try hard not to roll my eyes. It is clear to me now that it is not about the job—it never was—but rather about the family I will one day support with it. I pick at the tomatoes and peanuts, nodding my head every few seconds to show him I am listening this time.

———————————

A fourth memory.

I am eleven, writing a sixth-grade report on my parents' journey to this country in the early 1990s, and my dad tells me how he achieved the American Dream.

A dirt-covered farm boy who spent his childhood begging for leftover rice from street vendors, my dad worked harder than everyone else in his rural Henan province to leave it. He placed first on every placement exam until he became the only boy from his village to receive a scholarship to Tsinghua University (the "Harvard of China," he still calls it). There, he met my mom in orchestra class, where even after she rejected him twice, he pleaded to let him take her on a lunch date, where he finally wooed her by eating all the dumpling skins she peeled off so that she could have all the expensive pork inside. Later, as a couple, they protested against the Chinese government at Tiananmen Square in 1989, and my dad worked as a translator for American researchers who happened to be there at the same time. The researchers, impressed by his diligence and his English, gave him his ticket to America by offering to pay for his master's degree there.

Two years later, my dad began working twelve-hour night shifts at a Hartz Chicken Buffet while taking morning classes at Lamar University. My mom sent him money from her job in Hong Kong, and then in 1992, she flew to Texas to join him. They moved to Houston in 1995 to find new jobs and have my sister and me, and in 2003, they started their own company, Builders Club, to do the back-office work for local homebuilders and construction workers. As the face of this fledgling business thousands of miles away from home, my dad built himself a new life—one in which he was, once again, the smartest and hardest-working person in the room.

When my father cracks jokes about my career, I know he says even the worst things with love. But whereas I used to cry in response to his brutal honesty, I now egg him on.

When he glorifies the McKinseys and Goldman Sachses of the world, I'll tell him that my friends who currently work there all say they'd rather be me. When he tells me to study for law school, I tell him I'm too busy studying the laws of human nature instead for my second book.

"You're hopeless," he snapped at me one night when I told him I had just started my third revision of this essay.

"But it's about you!"

"If things were about me, you'd be doing other things with your life right about now."

"Ok, Dad, how about I just go back to finance for you." I threw it out as a joke, but like my dad, I am too serious not to actually consider it. Part of me—the one that worships Asian collectivism, risk aversion, and familial responsibility—still wonders if I should go chase his dreams. The other part—the one fueled by American individualism, unabashed curiosity, and "hopeless" romanticism—is always ready to fight back, going particularly berserk whenever my dad asks why I never want to be anything "more" than a writer or a teacher, anything that is *gāo yīdiǎn*—"higher?"

But after every bout of fighting and bantering comes a point when my dad finally runs out of breath and things to say, and I reach out my hand and place it on top of his. Even with the voices still clamoring in my head, I reassure my dad that I am listening to him. "Wǒ tīng dǒngle, bà," I say. *I understand.* At least, I am trying to.

So far, what I understand is my dad loves me but hates risks. He worries for my safety because of the hundred shores I could swim to, I am swimming toward shores I do not actually know if I can reach and that neither of us can see. I also understand dreams are not meant to be safe, but I struggle to explain this to someone who thinks my dreams are so elusive they do not—should not—exist in his world.

Sacrifice, responsibility, family—these are his world. I want to tell him they are mine, too, just not as he understands it.

We are trying, though, to understand each other. And with each new conversation we plunge into, he is less jarred by the splash, and I, the dive.

My dad is not the best at accepting my opinions; he is even worse at accepting my actions when they are not in line with what he thinks is best. But I know he means well. He always means well for those he loves, and I know this because each year on my mom's birthday, he buys her a cheesecake. My mom hates cheesecake, but he never fails to buy her one anyway because he loves cheesecake, and in fact thinks cheesecake is the best kind of cake, and he refuses to give her anything but the best—out of love, of course. This is how my dad loves me, too: seriously, selfishly, anxiously—the way he holds his feelings, the way he holds everything in this world dear to him.

My dad is learning to let go, or learning to try. Recently, in addition to ending our conversations with two impossible requests—to not to worry about him and to do only what makes me happy—he also observes that I have grown up, that I am more patient and now smarter than he ever was, and that he can no longer make all the decisions for me. He also thanks me for listening to him talk, at which point I realize only in the last two years have I let him talk like that—uninterrupted and the center of attention, like I am his.

So I think to myself, perhaps college worked after all: perhaps I am finally learning to let go too. To pursue my dreams, I must let go of the safety net he has cast for me. To be happy—both when I am sacrificing for family and when I am writing for myself—I must let go of his world and rebuild it as my own. Only then will I be able to make a living and make the ends meet: sacrifice, responsibility, family—but this time, my own.

And who knows? In a few years, or even a few decades, when this book has been sitting on the trophy shelf long enough to collect a thick layer of dust, after both of us have long forgotten the days I needed trophies to prove my potential, my dad will see me standing on a distant shoreline, waving, and he will smile and wave back. He will not try to save me when the tides come crashing in, he will not call after me to point out all the other shores I missed. Nor will he lecture me on making the right choices anymore, because all the choices—right and wrong—will have already been made on my own. As for who I end up becoming—a lawyer, a teacher, a CEO, a writer, or something neither of us could have foreseen—he will have no choice but to be proud of me. When he sees me, his daughter who breached unfamiliar waters to chase her dreams in the glimmering horizon, sunkissed and spent but happy, he might send a letter by sea that says something like, "Maybe you can make a living out of anything, after all."

HAD I GONE TO HARVARD

————

Had I gone to Harvard University, I would have fit right in as a self-proclaimed liberal arts nut. I would have taken Existentialism in Literature and Film and Empire, Nation, and Diaspora; I would have read *The Crimson* for good writing; I would have written for it, too. My most-read article would have been a confession on how I had grieved the gentrified aftermath of Cambridge Square, yet as a privileged university student, I had done little to stop it.

Had I gone to Harvard, I would not have majored in Economics and Sustainable Business—the two concentrations that brought me closest to the liberal arts at New York University's Stern School of Business. I still would have taken economics classes though. As a Harvard student, Adam Smith and his invisible hand would have turned me on in a wannabe-intellectual kind of way.

On the first day, I would have taken a brisk stroll across Harvard Yard to get to ECON101. I would not have run into a black man strutting down Fifth Avenue in a fishnet tank top and Barbie pink tights on my way there. Nor would I have lost track of time listening to homeless musicians bang on paint buckets and metal cups in Washington Square Park. And I certainly would not have had the absurd fear that, in my search for an NYU-designated building, I would somehow end up in SoHo's Forever 21 or at the Halloween store on Broadway between 11th and 12th Street, which sold bunny lingerie and rubber baby parts year-round.

At Harvard, I would have walked into the ECON101 lecture hall with a textbook written by Gregory Mankiw. I would have waited for Professor Mankiw to walk up to the lecture podium, only to realize Mankiw was too busy pumping out more textbooks in his office to teach his own class. With another nondescript white man teaching in his stead, I would learn to accept that Mankiw himself was the real invisible hand. After that, I would never care for another famous professor again. There would be too many to count, anyway.

At NYU, I was dazzled by no one. I had professors so horrible that I showed up only for my participation grade while reading books under the table. I also had professors who became lifelong friends. Jeffrey Younger and I shared lunch regularly at Quantum Leap; Jessy Hsieh and I discussed relationships and pet peeves over Mille-Feuille Bakery's lattes on LaGuardia Place. Somewhere along this spectrum were professors whose eccentricities simultaneously impressed and worried me, but, of course, they were hired by NYU not in spite of but because of these. (The head of the Business & Society Department, for instance, always started off his six-hundred-person freshman lecture course with a request for students to visit him in a Brooklyn warehouse on Tuesday nights, where he played lead guitarist in a three-person band.)

As for the ECON101 equivalent at NYU, I ended up in Paulson Auditorium with Simon Bowmaker, a professor well-known not for his textbooks but for his British accent, his photographic memory, and his ability to crack dad jokes in each class. After my semester with him, I decided to study economics at Stern. Three years later, we ran into each other again in the graduate school café.

"Amy, right?" he had asked as he poured hazelnut coffee into his cup. "It's been a while—how have you been?"

"Um, fantastic," I stuttered. "Even better now. How did you remember my name?"

"How could I forget? We talked a few times. And that nice little card you wrote me at the end of the semester—I still have it."

Had I gone to Harvard, I would have surprised no one. My sister went to Harvard. Her fiancé went to Harvard the year after. Her fiancé's sister went to Harvard two years after that, and now their youngest brother is trying to get in.

My sister tells me that, had I gone to Harvard, I would have enjoyed it.

"You probably would have lived at Canaday Hall your first year. It's the biggest one, and it's known for its crazy drunk Asian parties. You definitely would have gone to those. Maybe even blacked out at one or two."

I'll never know, of course, if I would have enjoyed Harvard. I'll never know how Canaday parties were, or how many I would have gone to, or if I would have blacked out at any. It is still hard for me to imagine what a college dorm party looks like because those kinds of parties did not exist at NYU. There was no campus, no "common room" to safely pass out in. At NYU, I partied, but I did so in places that were at least a 20-minute train ride away from where I lived—on

East Village rooftops and rooftop bars in Chelsea Piers, in the quiet suburbs of Jersey, in smoke-filled Koreatown clubs and gilded ballrooms of Midtown East, in Brooklyn basements where art studios by day were cleared out for lap dances at night. I never blacked out at any of them for fear of ending up on the wrong subway home. I sometimes wish I had, just to see what being trashed felt like, but then I remembered the nights where the police helped me carry my vomiting friends out of the train station into the December chill, and I promised myself I would never get to the point where someone questioned me to make sure I was okay, legally.

Had I gone to Harvard, attending parties would have been a way to blow off steam, to forget that during the week, my classmates and I were grains of rice stuck in a pressure cooker: boiled and compressed. Culled from the richest fields in the world—or so administration would boast—we would squirm and squeeze against each other in the hopes that, after four years of high heat and intense stress, we could pop out like the golden pellets they promised we would be. At least, this was how my sister described the pressure to excel to me. Parties, she said, had been a form of escapism from all that—a big fat middle finger to expectations and a drunken act of self-delusion. Parties were evidence that most Harvard students appeared golden on top but felt less so everywhere else.

My sister tells me I would have been stupefied by this chaos myself at the annual freshman Halloween party. Held in the basement of a research building and decorated like a low-budget EDM club, the First Chance Dance would have seemed less like a dance than an orgy of sweaty, half-naked teenagers in bejeweled lingerie and excessive body paint. I could have gone in wearing anything and still feel overdressed, but soon I'd be too drunk off jungle juice to care. With intense music and strobe lights washing out my soul, I'd weave my way to the center of the research lab, squeeze into the mosh pit of steaming, pungent bodies, and fit right in with everyone else.

Had I gone to Harvard, my freshman roommate might have developed depression from academic stress. My roommate at NYU developed depression for other reasons, the main one being that, having never left south Jersey before, she felt New York City was an industrial factory for loneliness. She rarely left the room and did work under the covers of her bed.

One time, I remember she popped out from her covers to tell me this: "Imagine going through college and never making a single friend. You could do that at NYU."

I believed her.

The only times I ever heard her speak louder than a whisper was at 3 a.m. on the weekends. I would wake up listening to her sob and scream at some "bitch" over the phone that "I hate it here and you don't understand" and "just shut up, shut up, shut up and listen!!!!"

A voice would crackle back on speaker phone. "I know, honey, I'm listening."

The bitch turned out to be her mom.

On her worst days, my roommate would lock me out of our room when she "needed to be alone."

Not wanting to end up another bitch in her life, I took these lockouts as unplanned opportunities to walk around Greenwich Village or catch the world falling asleep from our 5th Avenue rooftop. I remember spending hours watching the cars drive by in rivers of golden headlights and red tail-lights as dusk ate away the sky. Lost in the anonymity of it all, I would temporarily forget about my roommate and her depression and the locked room. I would forget how similar we felt some days—unwanted and alone. I would forget I had cried on college decisions day—not because NYU let me in but because Harvard, Princeton, Yale, The University of Chicago, and Columbia had thrown me out—which would have all been fine had I not seen my dad cry for the second time in my life and my mom keep asking my sister, "Why? Why? Why?"

I forgot about all of those locked rooms under the glow of the red Manhattan sun.

Had I gone to Harvard, I would not have fallen in love with the way the streetlights dance across skyscraper glass and the Brooklyn waterfront. I would not have entered a dorm raffle to see *The Lion King* musical, nor would I have won. I would not have woken up at 7 a.m. to line up for blue-berry pancakes smothered in maple butter cream down on Clinton Street. I would not have fallen asleep to Washington Park jazz on lazy Sunday afternoons. I would not have felt the intoxicating commotion of the Manhattan night reeling me in, its sirens echoing down the Avenues and promising that New York—with all its roaring messiness and unnerving chaos—would be beautiful.

Had I gone to Harvard, I would have expected everything to be beautiful—especially the people. I would have expected genius and been impressed by it until it made me numb. After running into daughters of TV personalities, princes from foreign countries, descendants of Kennedy, and heirs of Fortune 500 companies, I would find myself exhausted by the fame.

Had I gone to Harvard, I would have fantasized about the one or two times a year I could escape campus—parties and fame and all—and leave the Cambridge bubble behind. Sitting on the steps of the Widener Library, I would picture myself riding the Boston T into town, where after five stops on the Red Line, I'd hop off and walk to Chinatown. It would be nothing compared to the sprawling Chinatown community that spanned vast stretches of west Houston—endless blocks of apartment homes, shopping centers, dining plazas, parks, community buildings, art and dance and music schools, and churches—but I would not care.

After months of wading through red brick buildings and a sea of Harvard sweatshirts, anything farther away from the halls of ivy would feel a little closer to home. I'd get late-night dim sum at Hei La Moon or China Pearl and look out into the quiet evening streets illuminated by yellow lamp posts hanging like orbs in the winter fog. On my walk back to the T, I'd watch snow flurries drift past the shuttered doors of Gourmet Dumpling House, breathe in the scent of fried noodles mixed with the sharp night air, and promise to be back in this world again in two months, maybe three.

At NYU, late night outings rarely had that feeling of religious fervor. They were frequent, spontaneous, and occurred at every hour of the night thanks to a lack of apartment space and unlimited MetroCards.

I spent each weekend in a different place until I settled on a few favorites. Kenka on St. Mark's topped the list, what with its tanuki statues, Japanese graffiti, pink cinema advertisements, and 1970s exploitation movie posters of bondage and sex plastering the walls. Over the meaty sizzle of grills and the loud clinks of beer glasses, my friends and I would turn the izakaya into our own 2 a.m. short film for a while. If I didn't want to head down to St. Mark's, I'd stay in Koreatown eating soy garlic wings at Olive Chicken or drinking peach soju at Woorijip before a night of karaoke. And on Sunday nights, if dance practices in Jersey ended before 10 p.m., I'd head to Shaburo with some friends and share all-you-can-eat hotpot until closing time. On my way back to Manhattan, I'd sit in a window seat of the 167 bus and watch the Manhattan skyline twinkle across the Hudson. The city glowed from a distance, glittering under a light-polluted sky of violet and orange punctured by the spires of the World Trade Center and Empire State Building. I would watch the city like this before heading into the Lincoln Tunnel where, after a few seconds of darkness, I would emerge on 39th Street at 12th Avenue, suddenly a part of this pulsating world again.

Perhaps the only memory at Harvard that would have rivaled the surreality of late New York nights was Primal Scream. My sister told me that this was a tradition held the night before exams where I, along with hundreds of other Harvard students, would have gone outside in the December snow, drunk and wearing nothing but snow boots and a towel, counting down the seconds until midnight, at which point we'd throw off our coverings and begin running laps around the Yard naked, screaming "Sweet Caroline" at the top of our lungs while pushing past the sweaty butt cracks, flopping penises, hairy vaginas, oiled boobs, and lotioned legs of our peers. The band would be there in boxers and blazers, serenading us on, and the Chinese tourists who were still around would begin snapping pictures of us, mistaking this spirited cathartic release for a schoolwide porno. We would not mind their presence as we ran, given that our only sources of light were the occasional street lamp and their flash photography.

Had I gone to Harvard, I would have claimed that this hour-long event each year was the literal naked truth of the school. It was everything Harvard claimed to be and everything it abhorred: a unified student body, sweaty and naked and drunk and screaming, preparing for the onslaught of exams by running likely a fleshy herd of pale, slippery hippos through the night. We'd be a physical mass of inclusion and diversity, wasted and freezing and hugging each other to share the warmth of our naked bodies. Brown boobs, white asses, Hispanic pubes, Chinese dicks—they'd all look like one steaming blur in the frigid December air stripping away our breath and our stress. At some point, we would all end up in the middle of the Yard again, chanting "Harvard! Harvard! Harvard!" in group release. For a moment, nothing else would matter. For a moment, we would all be out of the pressure cooker.

Had I gone to Harvard, Primal Scream would have been the closest I got to defying my anxiety-ridden existence. It would have been a collective attempt to cure individual self-consciousness, an utterly un-Harvard-like exercise in escapism executed with the purest Harvard pride.

At NYU, no catharsis was ever so ritualistic. With no school spirit, no campus, no unifying class experiences other than orientation and graduation, we all had to develop our own Primal Screams. They were anywhere and everywhere in the city, instigated at random and usually by people I rarely knew. We were protagonists in our own movies, running madly in a city scintillating with cinematic presence. In the end, the absence of quiet nights made me more nostalgic for chaos than anything else.

Like my late-night outings, my cathartic experiences felt less like religious reckonings and more like rebellious acts of independence—the kind that taste sweeter when performed at random and alone. This happened once in Times Square. It was 5 in the morning, I could not sleep, and I ran from my apartment door to the Times Square Tower to watch the sun rise in the empty square around me. For once, the world was silent, and I stood there, breathing in untouched autumn air until the tourists began trickling in. On my way home, I jogged past flashing advertisements for CoverGirl mascara and Nike Air, $1 pizza stores and Victorian-era steakhouses, and street dancers warming up on Herald Square. I jogged past a man in a suit ordering ice cream for breakfast from the Wafels & Dinges cart in Greeley Park. I jogged past the Macy's that, at eleven stories tall and a whole block wide, held the title of "the world's largest store." I lived right across from this Macy's. I stepped into the lobby of Herald Towers, face flushed and out of breath, and when the doorman saw me, grinning, he delivered the following question as a statement of fact: "Great day to be in New York, huh."

On college T-shirt day four years ago, I remember feeling nauseated. I remember putting on a shirt that said NYU Stern and spending the rest of the day explaining to people that Stern was the name of a business school I never thought I would go to. I remember crying at lunch, confessing to my best friend Lauren that I felt like I had let everyone down, especially my parents, because I was not in the Harvard T-shirt they expected to see.

"Yes, I suppose we did expect you would get into Harvard," Lauren said. "But I'm so glad you didn't." I blinked.

"What I mean is," she quickly went on, "if anyone could prove that you can do college right anywhere and be just fine, it would be you."

Of course, neither of us knew what "doing college right" meant at the time—no high schooler did. As it turned out, college was not about doing things right at all but doing things, period, and seeing what happened next. College was an interim playground for infinite trial runs, for Primal Screams that helped me better understand my own.

In the end, my own Primal Scream was very much like a nerve-racking streak in the dark. It was a messy sprint through the fog, a psychedelic confluence of unexpected events saturated with a dreamlike quality. It was a course in self-awareness for which the world was my teacher and the curriculum changed day by day. The end result of it all was not a diploma or letter grade but a rough embrace of an unfinished truth. That truth was this: I could have gone to college anywhere and emerged with a voice richer and more resonant than what came before.

The voice I have now is the only one I know. It is also everything I know. Had I gone to Harvard, my voice would have belonged to someone else. Who that person might have been, I'll never know. I still think about her from time to time, but only in the way one thinks of a past lover: briefly and in passing. Whereas just four years ago, I would have done anything to speak with her voice, I would do anything to keep the one I have now.

My high school friend knows this too. Somehow, she knew all along. In my third year at NYU, I called Lauren late one night to tell her that she had been right. College, New York, and everything that came with it had ended up being just fine. Better than fine, actually. It became home.

ON TAKING CARE OF PETS

———

Never name a dog Lucky unless you want her to bite you in the ass.

My parents brought Lucky home one day when I was just three years old. She was a black Labrador puppy and our first family pet. A business client of theirs had given her up, claiming he was too busy to care for a dog. We found out years later he was only busy because he had been running a failed Ponzi scheme and was $500,000 in debt, but at the time, all my parents knew was this puppy was in need of a home, and they were willing to provide one. Unfortunately, they had no idea how to take care of her.

Instead of micromanaging Lucky like they did with my sister and me, my parents thought the best way to love a dog was to let her be—wild and carefree in the backyard— where she spent her time chasing her own tail, chewing on gardening tools, and eating our greasy sausage leftovers and anything else she killed under the old oak trees. My sister and I grew up going to piano lessons and dance rehearsals; Lucky grew up pursuing what my parents imagined was a life of liberty and doggy happiness.

Had I been old enough, I would have chided my parents for never sending Lucky to obedience school or feeding her a balanced diet. I would have trained her not to shit on top of the grill, and I would have let her indoors some days, particularly on the steaming summer afternoons where Texas-sized mosquitoes swarmed in black clouds.

Alas, at three years old, I had neither the moral attentiveness nor the vocabulary to convince my parents that we were loving Lucky in all the wrong ways. I was too self-absorbed to realize I was part of the problem, too. Given how aggravatingly needy I was, I suspect my parents' attention toward me underpinned their negligence toward Lucky. I wish it had not been an either-or situation, but in the end, I was their daughter, and Lucky was their dog, and my parents could only put up with so much from either.

At some point, Lucky must have realized she would never be able to outbid me for attention. In defiance, she began practicing her high jump in the backyard until one day, she leapt straight over our seven-foot wooden fence and into the neighbor's pool. No matter how many times the neighbors threw her out, she kept going back. My parents finally decided to give Lucky away once she started spending more time in other people's backyards than our own. Our increasingly irritated block of neighbors helped with the flyers.

"2-year-old black Labrador up for adoption," they said. "High energy. Goofy smile. Loves swimming and smoked sausages."

We ended up giving Lucky to a family friend who just so happened to be looking for a dog when we needed to get rid of one. A few weeks later, that friend called to tell us that Lucky had gotten so excited on a morning walk that she broke out of her leash, ran up to a policeman who was making rounds that day, and bit him in the ass. When we asked if the policeman and Lucky were okay, the friend told us that the policeman was fine, but Lucky had already been sent to the pound and put down.

"Lucky was a good dog," my mom tried to reason while my sister and I cried. "She was a good dog. Very big heart. Just unlucky." And so Lucky's fate was blamed on bad luck as opposed to irresponsibility, and we all moved on.

In the third grade, I convinced myself that I could handle a new pet. I decided to ask my parents for three Chinese dwarf hamsters after seeing how cute they were throwing wood shavings at each other in our local PetSmart. To demonstrate how responsible I was, I did some research beforehand.

A quick Google search the night before my proposal taught me all I needed to know. First, Chinese dwarf hamsters, otherwise known as *Cricetus griseus*, made for "great first pets" because, unlike Lucky, they were "easy to handle." Second, these hamsters needed only five hundred square inches of living space and eight inches of bedding to dig around in (translation: not as messy as a dog), required only an exercise wheel to stay happy and fit (translation: not as needy as a dog), grew to only about five centimeters in length and two ounces in weight (translation: much cheaper to feed than a dog), and lived an average life of three years (translation: much less likely to wreak havoc than a dog, statistically speaking). Most importantly, I stressed to my parents that if havoc were in fact wreaked, I would take full responsibility.

The next weekend, I came home with three hamsters, ready to begin my career as an animal social worker. With newfound confidence, I introduced my furry little creatures to the family. I told my sister they were like three younger brothers except better because they never cried and couldn't talk back.

For a while, each day after school consisted of hamster play dates during which I would watch them spin on their wheel, comment on their perfectly round poop, or poke their giant balls thinking they were bright pink butts. A few peaceful months passed like this in the Dong household—I had just about proven my proficiency in pet care.

Then, one afternoon as I was refilling their water bottle, I felt an itchy sensation on my ankle. A plump black speck was bouncing around on my left sock. I caught it, squeezed it until I heard a little crunch, and brought the bloody specimen to my parents. Upon seeing the dead bug on my index finger, my dad ran out of the room and straight for the hamster cage. "Fleas!" I heard him call from the living room. "NIÁNG XǏ PÌ!" *FUCKING SHIT.* "These little buggers are giving us FLEAS!"

My dad loaded my hamsters into the back of his pickup truck that night and told my sister and me he'd be back in an hour. When I asked my mom where he was taking them, she simply said, "Far, far away from here." At that moment, I knew I had failed my newly adopted family members. My hamsters had been betrayed not by fleas, then, but by my own ineptitude—my horrific inability to take care of the things I loved.

As the three of them were driven off into the distance, I wondered if there were such thing as a hamster pound. I settled on hamster heaven instead: that sounded better, and it made me—the uptight eight-year-old who had prematurely taken full responsibility for the disappearance of three innocent lives—feel better, too.

The cat came next. Her name was Mimi or Mia or something like that—I don't remember anymore because we only had her for one night.

In our desperation to prove we could take care of yet another pet, my sister and I somehow convinced our parents to get us a cat in spite of our dander allergies. The night we brought Mimi/Mia home, I stroked her for five minutes before spending the next twelve hours lying in bed wheezing, crying, and stuffing tissue paper up my nostrils to stop a nosebleed. Mimi/Mia was clearly allergic to me, too, because the next morning when I came out into the living room with my face still swollen, I watched her projectile vomit a chunky, orange-yellow stream of Meow Mix and leftover fried chicken into the fireplace before collapsing into a trembling ball.

My parents drove Mimi/Mia three hours back to the breeding ranch they got her from and handed her to a confused old man. She had cost $150, but apparently, my parents did not get a refund, not even a partial one. When I later asked them why not, they glared at me and snapped, "Because we were too embarrassed to ask."

My last mammalian pet was a Rex rabbit named Jenny. We adopted her from the rescue center at PetSmart after we found out they had run out of hypoallergenic cats.

In addition to having a black back, a white tummy, and a brown diamond on her forehead, Jenny came with a big fat attitude. In the year we cared for her, she taught my family three things: First, rabbits enjoy ripping apart paper with their maxillary incisors. Second, rabbits demonstrate disapproval by emitting short, guttural grunts. Third, rabbits betray you by running away.

Jenny produced her own escape hatch by biting through the backyard playpen we had made her from welded, galvanized steel. The first time she slipped through, we ran after her down the block and caught her with a big black fishing net. The second time, we didn't even notice when she left. She simply disappeared into the tangerine Texas sunset, scurrying into the distance and probably grunting the whole way. After holding onto her cage for a week, I gave up my search and unceremoniously declared Jenny roadkill. As with every pet I'd had before, I ended our relationship with a half-guilty, half-angry farewell that only made me more determined to find my next loving companion.

After Jenny, I swore off all animals with hair, as well as any other animal that might fill me with moral dread if it were to die under my care. I was a good person—the world needed to know this, and I was also desperate to prove it to myself. That left me with three options: fish, amphibians, and insects. I started with fish.

Instead of buying them at a pet store like a normal person, I captured mine each year at the Lunar New Year festival in Chinatown, where you could pay three dollars to squat at a booth and play a thirty-second all-you-can-catch game scooping goldfish out of an inflatable kiddy pool. I'd catch five or six and appoint myself their guardian angel before a more careless child could. Back home, I fed them gourmet pellets, bought them expensive decorations, and neurotically cleaned their glass bowl each week. But without a fish tank or filter, it wasn't long before they all decided to go belly up. I flushed them down the toilet when that happened, apologizing to them one by one for not being good enough.

Amphibians came next. After a night of heavy rain, I scooped tadpoles from street gutters. My tadpoles and I were masters of roleplay: I was the animal rescuer from the Houston SPCA; they were the abandoned babies given a second chance at life. I gave them a beautiful view of my elementary school fruit paintings through their Tupperware container, the aquarium decorations left over from my fish days, and juicy bloodworms I purchased as frozen cubes and later thawed to the perfect temperature. Once I had gotten involved in their lives to quite an intimate degree, I named them. Bill was the shy one. Little Bean—my childhood nickname—was the fat one. Swirly always flaunted the beautiful spiral pattern on his stomach, and Timmy, Tad, and Taddy acted like their own middle school clique— brooding, angsty, and snappy when anyone else popped their personal bubble.

Over the course of two weeks, my tadpoles all grew legs. Soon, Little Bean and Tad began resembling muddy, wart-covered toads. And they might have one day had little Tads of their own had I not forgotten to refill their water before leaving for a three-day excursion at Galveston Beach. When I got back, I found a few gray smudges on their sand floor that I assumed were the bodies of the slain. Little Bean and Tad were nowhere to be found—perhaps they had crawled out of the holes in the saran wrap I kept over the bowl. Perhaps they managed to hop to the nearest window, unlatch the safety lock, and dive into the great big world. Perhaps the toads croaking outside my window now are their great-great-great-great-great-great-grandchildren.

I turned to insects last. Because everyone else hated them, I was determined to love them. They were my last hope for salvation. If I could prove to myself that I could look past their horrid features and raise them like my own children, I would be able to pardon everything of the past. I could picture it perfectly: the *Houston Chronicle* article they would write about me, Amy Dong, the compassionate activist who preached equality not only among all genders and races but also between all species—even the blood-curdling and blood-sucking ones.

My house spider George came first. George was cute until he got too picky. I spent hours killing fruit flies and easing them into the plastic water bottle I kept him in, but George never showed me any appreciation. I assumed he preferred his prey alive rather than looking like withered raisins, but there was only so much he could ask of me. But ask he did, and when I could not deliver, he spun a web so thick I couldn't see him anymore. After I could no longer determine whether he was alive or not, I threw the water bottle away.

I tried ants next, scooping a couple dozen from my backyard into an open plastic bin. But after I woke up one morning and found a few crawling on my bed, I ran screaming from the room, promising never to intrude upon their livelihoods again.

I ended up feeling the greatest affection for my cockroaches, Philip and Fred. They had been scrounging around in the kitchen, homeless and famished, when I took them into my care by gently swatting them into a glass jar that once held canned pears. As I poked air holes in the metal lid to give them sufficient oxygen, I reassured them that I was not the cockroach exterminator. On the contrary, I was their savior.

"Love me and I will love you back," I whispered as I placed them under my bed.

But Philip and Fred did not seem to understand our deal. Even though I fed them Werther's Original caramels, rotting fruit, and honeyed water every day, they kept trying to climb to the top of their jar and run away. They twitched their antennae in disdain when I lifted them up to look outside the window, and they did nothing at all when I came home from school to tell them about my day.

"Philip, Fred—listen carefully now: history is a hard subject. Don't let anyone tell you otherwise. You guys are lucky you can just sit here all day and have a siesta whenever you want. I don't have that luxury. No, between doting on you two and memorizing the battles of World War II, I barely have time to sleep."

One day after school, I walked over to their jar and was hit with a horrible stench. When I unscrewed the lid, I learned something no one had ever bothered to tell me before: cockroaches *reek*. Worse than spoiled cottage cheese or week-old garbage, Philip and Fred smelled like something terrifying and intangible—something like depression, or treachery, or grief.

I didn't know what to do with them after that. I didn't want to let them go; I was afraid they'd forget about me. I didn't want to keep them; they would permanently damage my sense of smell. I didn't want to kill them by flushing them down the toilet, either, because that would make me miss my goldfish.

Finally, I decided to send them off "Last Supper" style. I placed two pieces of baguette bread inside their jar, filled it three-quarters of the way with water, and slowly watched their beautiful brown bodies sink beneath the water line as they tore into their soggy meal with twitching antennae and jagged jaws. When they started performing underwater acrobatics, I brought their jar to the trash can and, with teary eyes, asked them to forgive me.

After a lifetime of murdering animals of all sizes, shapes, colors, and backgrounds, I took a brief hiatus from pet care and instead spent that time taking better care of myself. Save for an eating disorder and a few anxiety attacks here and there, I'd say I've been pretty successful at enjoying life.

But whether it's boredom, the extra down time I have from being quarantined by COVID-19, or my maternal instincts kicking in a bit too early, I want to give pet ownership another go.

Maybe one day, I'll get myself some chickens.

To make them the perfect home, I'll build a spacious chicken coop with elevated wire that runs deep into the ground and forms a rooftop that neither hawks nor possums can break into. I'll let my chickens roam cage-free during the day and let them sleep in an incubated nest at night. I'll set out water trays and buy chicken feed in case weeds, grass clippings, and bugs alone aren't enough. I'll plan, build, and watch over this home so that nothing can go wrong.

Or maybe everything will go wrong anyway, because somehow I never take care of my pets as well as I believe I can.

Last month, my mom told me I could buy some young hens if I promised to let her harvest the eggs. I called our local chicken farm and wrote down the address and the opening hours, but I have not done anything since then. Perhaps I know that if I visit, I will buy a dozen hens and take them home and raise them and, in the process of doing so, end up killing them one by one. If that happens, I worry that I may feel unfit to take care of anything at all. Chickens would be the last straw, and as someone who wants children, I wouldn't be able to bear that truth.

If I do choose to have children one day, I hope they turn out okay. I hope that, as a child who failed to take care of her pets, I can still make things right with my kids. This time, I will give them sufficient space to roam, as well as extracurriculars that consist of more than ripping paper and running on wheels. I hope my children will never turn to a diet of rotting fruit and soggy bread, but that they instead enjoy balanced meals of patience, reassurance, and affection, sprinkled with an occasional pinch of danger.

Whatever the case may be, I know my children will demand more attention than all of my previous pets combined. Hasty Google searches won't cut it. Health problems and fleas can't be shipped off. Disobedience can't be flushed down the toilet, and absolutely nothing can be drowned. While our time together was short-lived, my previous pets are searing reminders that, if I ever decide to have children, I had better prepare to love and care for them like my own life depends on it. Because if not, Lucky will surely be tossing in her grave, laughing when my own children bite me in the ass one day.

OYSTER OMELETS IN SINGAPORE

———

I sat still in the sticky humid heat—the kind that slows down time, particularly at night—and took in the neon-lit hawker stalls of Singapore that stayed crowded past midnight. I licked satay sauce off a barbecue sambal stingray bone, waiting for the man at stall 73 to fry up my oyster omelet.

It was my second day here as an exchange student at the National University of Singapore, and having flown here alone, I felt comforted being surrounded by everything familiar to me: the emphatic, slurred voices of almost-drunk students, the red and gold Chinese characters framing English words, and the clattering plates of roast duck rice being shuffled family style. Unrestrained laughter rippled through the air, reminding me that dinner was the best meal of the day because there was always someone to eat it with.

Of course, everything was different too. I listened to Malaysian, Indonesian, Indian, and Chinese families comfortably jabbering in a mix of English and their home languages. I walked past stalls serving dishes that were distant cousins of my family's: *char kway teow* instead of hand-pulled beef noodles, chili crab instead of steamed scallion and ginger tilapia. I watched people separate red trays from green because the latter meant "halal only," but despite how strange all these elements seemed, I knew I was the stranger.

Only the oyster stall owner knew who I was: Customer Number 28. It was a temporary identity, a receipt of friendly exchange. I would be replaced by others tomorrow. Tonight, I was just a starry-eyed stranger in this place, a number in a queue, a transient visitor to be greeted and then sent on her way. I was a bubble floating through space, hovering quietly as I observed the world around me. Every smell, every taste, every breath—it was all unimaginable in the most literal sense. Just two days ago, I could not have foreseen myself sitting here, chewing on stingray bones as I acquainted myself with hawker centres and humid Singapore air.

Sudden shouts from the prata and chicken rice stalls startled me. A stall worker rushed by, and with him came the hefty waft of Tiger lager and peanut dipping sauce. I took a deep breath. If I truly was alone in a foreign place, that meant I was free. I was a slate that, once covered in twenty-one years of powdered chalk, had suddenly and soundlessly been wiped clean. I was not afraid to write or be written on. Tonight, I was Number 28; tomorrow, anything.

"Number 28!" the beady-eyed man called for me then, as if on cue.

"Jiùshì wǒ," I announced as I walked up to his stall. *That's me.* His eyes grew round, glowing like the neon signs above his head that read: HUP KEE FRIED OYSTER OMELETTE, Stall 73.

"Nǐ búshì zhèlǐ de rén ba?" he asked excitedly. *You're not from here, are you?*

"Bú shì," I blushed. "Wŏ shì láizì mĕiguó de liúxuéshēng." *I'm an American exchange student.* "Dànshì wŏ fùmŭ shì zhōngguó rén." *But my parents are Chinese.* I stated the second part with gusto, as if I were displaying proof of kinship. He grinned and replied in Mandarin, "Ah, I see, I see, that explains your funny accent. It didn't sound local, but it didn't sound mainland Chinese, either." He asked if I wanted extra scallions as he slid an omelet onto a Styrofoam plate. I nodded.

"You know," he continued as he dashed them on, "I can see the American in you now. Your eyes, so big. Very full of emotions, very animated. Your clothes too. Bold, American, very bright and colorful." The line grew long behind me. He went on like he either hadn't noticed or didn't care.

"You like Singapore so far?" he continued.

"It's beautiful."

"I hope so. More beautiful than America?" he chuckled, as if laughing at an inside joke. "How is it, growing up there? Is it as good as they say it is? You know, Singapore is growing now too. May be better than America one day. But still, you are very lucky to be American. Smart, too, for eating here," he pointed at my tray and grinned. "So what made you want to come to Singapore?"

The kitchen staff called him back before I could respond. "Nàme duō rén dĕng zhene, nĭ gàn ma ne?" *So many people are waiting. What are you doing?*

"Āiyā, láile láile!" *Coming, coming!* The man shuffled back behind his oil-splattered wall once more. As he began frying the omelets for Customers Number 29 and 30, he started humming to an old Chinese song I recognized but had not heard since childhood. We stood facing each other for a few seconds, sketching out each other's identities until I began walking away with my tray.

"Xièxiè!" I thanked him. He lifted his spatula and waved, spraying a new coat of hot yellow oil onto his screen.

Back in my seat, I stared at the orbs of fried oysters winking at me from their Styrofoam chaise. Silver and gray and black stripes wrapped around their translucent bodies like marbled tapioca pearls. I poked at the oyster lying on top of the heap with my fork. It half slid, half tumbled down to the bottom, nestling itself into the folds of the egg like a buoy floating in a chrome-colored sea. The other oysters lay undisturbed, pressed cozily against each other in their delicate mold. Each was a world of its own, unaware when others settled in or slipped away.

I pierced the lone oyster through its center and brought it to my mouth. The pearl popped messily as I bit down. The taste of bittersweet seawater burst on my tongue before the briny flesh of the body cut through. The spice of the scallions followed, and the fragrance of sesame-oiled yolk came last, washing my anticipation down with it. *This is what an oyster omelet tastes like,* I told myself as I swallowed. I lowered the anchor into memory before tearing away at the rest of the egg. I left the remaining oysters to the side—I had preferred the stingray.

I didn't regret ordering it, nor did I hate the taste. I was aware only of the fact that the omelet had neither exceeded nor fallen short of my expectations because I had had none. There had been nothing to compare it to, which was what made ordering it so tempting in the first place.

And this, I realized, was what made traveling alone so appealing—the ability to live without expectation. Sitting in this hawker centre, a stranger by choice, I was convinced there was nothing like chasing adrenaline in the new. As I ate and drank the night away, I also knew this: if to travel was to acknowledge another's world, to dine in one was to appreciate that it exists.

I wished I had come to these conclusions two years ago when I first studied abroad in Europe. I was a sophomore in college then, and after spending four months at New York University's campus in Prague along with all of my other business school friends, I came home not with a revelation of self but a performance of one. One professor of mine, Mark Brennan, later exposed my charade. The entire NYU Study Away program, he explained, was a sham.

"Studying at one of NYU's global sites," he once told me after class, "is the equivalent of living in my classroom and taping a sign that says 'Prague' outside the door. You speak in English. You hang out only with other NYU students. You learn nothing about the real world. It's all the same. Except the classroom option is cheaper."

It was not courage, then, but embarrassment that brought me back abroad. I came to Singapore alone to experience the unmistakable authenticity of lives I had supposedly evaded in Europe. How curious it was to feel that one night of accidents in Singapore had trumped a month of routine in Prague.

As the evening carried on, a few families began trickling out the main entrance. The tables adjacent to me emptied, but I was determined to stay. I wanted to watch over everything for as long as I could: the full yellow moon hanging in the sky, the triangular flags flapping overhead in a festive blur of crisscrossing lines, the rainbow lights casting an iridescent shadow on the last of the late-night crowd.

It was not until after I took a Grab taxi home that I realized where I had been all along. The brown gable roof, the round stools and long rectangular tables, the open-seating area marked by streamers of orange and white and pink and green: it was the hawker centre that had been featured in the romantic comedy *Crazy Rich Asians*. In the movie, the main character Rachel Chu was, like me, a young Chinese-American seeing Singapore for the first time. She also lived in New York City and had ties to NYU. Upon her arrival, she also chose to dive, to sink, to embrace her new reality. And the first thing she did was to come here and dine at the historic Newton Food Centre.[7]

Though I had spent the past two hours pretending to be no one, my charade fell apart as I suddenly began missing my home and my family. *Crazy Rich Asians* was the first English movie we had watched together in seven years. My parents had been the ones who demanded to see it when they heard it featured an Asian-American family.

After the movie ended, my mom had asked for a family photo. As we lined up in front of the movie poster, she said, "Maybe one day we can go and eat all that food too!"

I realized now she had been talking about the scene at Newton Food Centre where Rachel was sharing satay skewers, beer, popiah, and chili crab with her new friends. A part of me wished that my family were here to relive that scene with me; another part was glad they were not. I felt a peculiar joy in having tried these things by myself. It was a selfish feeling, but it was the truth.

My recollection of watching *Crazy Rich Asians* with my family gave me a sense of renewed urgency to travel independently, at least for a little while longer. It was a beautiful

---

7   *Crazy Rich Asians*, directed by Jon M. Chu (Burbank, CA: Warner Bros. Home Entertainment, 2018), film.

thing, to feel content in a stranger's home. It was a rarity to live with no identity and no past. Of course, I knew I would have to reclaim both in the end.

But for now, I welcomed the solitude. I also questioned it, wondering if solo travel could ever make me feel truly alone. If my world was an oyster, it was nestled against millions of others, all forming the same kinds of pearls as mine at any moment.

MY MOTHER VOTED FOR TRUMP

If New York City is the epicenter of liberal thought, New York University is both its beacon and its breeding ground. In college classes, at club events, and on the streets, the only two political thoughts ever shared openly are this: first, that Trump is an ugly son of a bitch, and second, that the only thing uglier than his appearance is his soul.

In my four years at NYU, I agreed with the first statement mostly for its entertainment value. For some reason, it was intensely satisfying to describe Trump as a burnt nacho cheese chip with a wig bleached and fried to a Barbie Blond, a mouth puckered as if it were permanently sucking on a sour Warhead, and a face so orange and swollen it seemed that at any second it would erupt into a minefield of Cheetos-colored acne.

As for the second statement, I agreed partly out of solidarity and partly out of fear. I disliked Trump for all the reasons everyone else did, but I also disliked that my classmates and professors shamed those who "did not despise him enough," conflating their pro tempore behavior with immutable and unforgivable identities. In their eyes, every

Trump sympathizer was a racist or a sexist or a single-minded bigot. Supporters did not just make ignorant remarks; they were ignorant, period.

So I went through my four years of NYU deliberately hiding the fact that my mother voted for Trump in 2016. If my own friends believed that Trump supporters were "idiots who shouldn't be allowed to have kids" and "unbelievably selfish assholes," what would they have thought of her?

In the sixth grade, I wrote a report on my parents' journey to America. As I interviewed them, my mom taught me an important life lesson.

"Always stand up for what you believe in, Amy," she said in Mandarin. I nodded.

"I know—"

"Wait, I wasn't finished." She cleared her throat and started again. "Always stand up for what you believe in, Amy—unless, of course, you're trying to stand up against China, in which case it's useless, and you're better off booking a one-way ticket to anywhere else in the world and getting the fuck out of that rat hole before the communists kill you."

This was how she started her immigration story. How she, a well-off, accomplished student at Tsinghua University—the Harvard of China—became a fugitive in search of freedom. How she ran from Beijing to Beaumont, Texas, with nothing except her pride, her grit, and her trust in the elusive American Dream.

My mother fled China after tanks tried to kill her at the Tiananmen Square protests in 1989. Both she and my dad had been there that day on June Fourth to protest the death of pro-reform officer Hu Yaobang and to call for democracy, freedom of the press, freedom of speech, and constitutional due process.

"It was so disorganized," my mom said. "We were all twenty-year old college kids trying to change the world. We didn't know it was impossible. It didn't feel impossible when hundreds of thousands of other people were there with us. We all wanted freedom. That day, we felt we were closer to it." Her face had a distant look to it.

"And then the army came," she said. "It was early morning. All the lights in the square went off. We heard gunshots. We saw giant shadows coming for us. Those were the tanks. Your dad and I were already running for the trees when they started firing at us. We only looked back once. We saw his classmate getting gunned down."

That day soon became known as the Tiananmen Massacre. It was the culmination of what some people now call the '89 Democracy Movement.

I tried to picture it: my Democrat-hating mother standing up to an entire government to plea for democracy. I tried to imagine her standing in that square, swallowed in a crowd of angry, hungry college students, believing if she shouted long and hard enough into the early morning wind, the Chinese government would stop and listen.

"Deng Xiaoping and Li Peng sent the People's Liberation Army to bring back peace," my mom said bitterly. "What peace? What liberation? We were pigs for slaughter. They wanted our heads because we were finally lifting them to speak up."

I did not know what to say after that. I, for one, had never before risked my life for an intangible belief.

"Is that why you came here?" I asked, changing the subject instead. "To America? To Texas?"

"Yes. Around that time, your dad worked as an English translator for some researchers from Lamar University. After the protests, they offered him the opportunity to come to America and get his master's degree at Lamar. They said they wanted to pay him back for his work with a scholarship. He said he would think about it. Back then, your dad was a poor man from a rural village. He did not want to leave his family in Henan—he was afraid to lose his home. He told me if we stayed, he had a good chance of becoming a rich government official one day. But I told him we had to go. I said to him, 'If you do not leave now, you will lose everything anyway, you will see.' I told him I would be the first to leave."

And so my dad came to America with $200—his entire family's savings—tucked away in his coat pocket. He landed in California thinking Texas was close by, but when a friend picked him up at the airport and gave him a map, he booked the cheapest Greyhound he could find and stayed awake the entire trip to make sure he got off at the right stop. My mother came to join him two years later; she had gone first to Hong Kong to work and send money to him. Together, as my dad completed his master's, they worked as a fry cook at a fried chicken buffet and a waitress at a Chinese restaurant to pay the bills. After he graduated, they scraped together enough money to move to Houston, where they rented a one-bedroom apartment and started working for a wealthy Chinese homebuilder who agreed to sponsor their green cards. Seven years later in 2000, they took out a mortgage on a small office building and started their own company, Builders Club Services, Inc., where they still work to this day.

While my mother was a rowdy and an outspoken activist in China, she became a shy and private person in America. Even though she has been speaking English for over two decades, she is still so embarrassed by her accent that she asks me to order at restaurants for her. She never speaks in public unless she has to. When the neighbors greet us, she motions for me to hold them off in conversation until she can run back indoors.

Not that my mom does not want friends—she simply does not want enemies. Even when I wrote the report about her in sixth grade, she had been hesitant to share her immigration story with me for fear that a Chinese person would hear it and send the *Gòngchǎndǎng*, the Chinese Communist Party, after her.

"It does not matter that we are in America. They will still track us down."

So of course, when I told my mom that I wanted to write an essay about her, she was furious.

"Don't you even think about it, Amy Dong," she threatened.

"But I *have* to, mom. Your story is powerful. It's different."

"What a load of mǎ pì." *Horse farts.* "Chòu háizi. Bèndàn. Shǎguā." *Stinky kid. Stupid egg. Silly melon.* She stopped making her chive and egg pancakes and wagged a flour-covered rolling pin at my face with every angry syllable. When I started laughing, she chased me around the counter until every Mandarin epithet she could think of was exhausted and an angry cloud of flour had formed around her.

"You think this is funny, but this is serious," she coughed. "You make fun of me enough in front of your friends. Now you want to expose me to the world? If you write about me in your book, everyone will know what we think."

"Maybe that's a good thing."

"I'm never telling you anything ever again."

A few days later, she let me interview her anyway. She called me a nosy bean each time I asked a question, but her constant laughter told me she was enjoying herself. Perhaps she felt happy, or simply relieved, that after years of bickering, I was finally listening and trying to understand.

———

What I am still trying to understand is how my mom can hate Xi Jinping for mistreating his people and love Trump for doing the same. I am trying to understand how one of these men is the devil and the other is a saint—how one is the reason she left a country and the other is the reason she stayed.

Both Donald Trump and Xi Jinping are demagogues. The former wants to "strongly regulate, or close down" parts of the Internet; the latter employs thousands of people to enforce restricted access.[8] The former wants his lawyers "to make complaints disappear"; the latter makes people themselves disappear.[9] The former detains protesters and illegal immigrants in prison; the other exiles Xinjiang Uyghurs to

---

8   Shannon Bond and Avie Schneider, "Trump Threatens To Shut Down Social Media After Twitter Adds Warning To His Tweets," NPR, May 27, 2020.

9   "The Lawsuits of Donald Trump," *The Atlantic*, March 20, 2013.

modern-day concentration camps.[10] Both men thrive under despotic rule; Xi Jinping simply thrives more because, in his country, his word is law.

But my mom tells me it is simple to understand, really.

"I love Trump because Trump hates Xi Jinping," my mom explained to me at dinner one day. "Nothing else matters."

"What do you mean, nothing else matters?"

"Trump is a strong man. A fighter. He speaks his mind and does not care what people think about him. That is freedom. That is—what do you call it in English?—freedom of speech."

"You don't understand," I pleaded with her. "Trump is divisive. He's tearing this country apart. His law and order rhetoric is terrifying. You ran *away* from law and order! How can you love it here?"

"No, *you* don't understand," she snapped back. "This country is beautiful. Laws protect you, not kill you. You work hard, you get a job, you say whatever you want to say and someone listens."

"Not if you're black or Hispanic or a woman or an immigrant."

"No! Trump loves us hard-working immigrants. We make the economy strong."

"Ma, he calls the pandemic the China virus."

"Yes, I know. I like that name. It makes perfect sense—China *is* a virus. China is a dà huàidàn." *A big evil egg.* "And all Trump is doing is exposing the belly. He's exposing Chinese corruption. Telling the truth."

"I don't think Trump cares for telling the truth."

---

10 "Data leak reveals how China 'brainwashes' Uighurs in prison camps," BBC, November 24, 2019.

"What do you know?" my mom exploded, slamming her chopsticks down on the table. "You grew up here, where truth is what *you* want it to be. You did not grow up in China. There, they tell you what the truth is. If you do not believe in their truth, they get rid of you. I came here to decide my own truth. And my truth is that I believe in Trump. He is brave, you know? Like a soldier. Xi Jinping cannot bully him like he bullies everyone else. Trump is the only one who can stand up to him—to evil. And you will never change my mind about that."

"You're just as stubborn as Trump is."

"Yes, and I love that! We will finally get China to change its ways. All the economic sanctions and visa bans and threats for World War III—we need that. I learned the hard way that words are no use. Only action. And Trump is a man of action. He will stand up for what is right."

Stand up for what is right—the same thing my mom told me ten years ago when she explained why she had risked her life for a political ideal. When my mom said this again, I thought of her standing in the middle of Tiananmen Square at six in the morning, a nineteen-year-old shouting to whomever would listen to her, standing up for what she thought was right until she could not stand anymore.

I decided to let it go. Perhaps my mom was right—I do not know much.

"Ma, do you know this English saying—the enemy of my enemy is my friend?"

"Yes."

"You embody it perfectly."

"Thank you."

When my mother talks about America, she is talking about her freedom of speech and her protected constitutional rights and the promise that no one is above the law. When she cites Trump's message for "law and order," she is calling not for federal troops to gun down protesters, but for citizens and their government to champion and protect democracy.

To my mother, China and America, Xi Jinping and Trump—they are all just symbols in her head.

She still dreams of that pitch-black morning in Tiananmen Square, where classmates and strangers were shot dead around her, where her dreams were crushed by the country she thought was home.

Now, when I argue about politics with my mom, I also try my best to understand: What it is like to have one's home destroyed overnight. What it is like to feel betrayed by the people who raised you. What it is like to run away with no language, no money, and nothing to guide you but the fear of everything that came before. I am trying to understand my mother's hatred, but understanding such a powerful emotion without sharing her past is hard.

If I try hard enough, I think that maybe, if I were my mother, I would vote for Trump too. I would vote for him because he would hate the Chinese government almost as much as I did. I would vote for him not because I was blind to his racism or sexism, but because my hatred for China would be more powerful than the truth. And I would voice my bitterness in 2016, in 2020, and for however long afterward at the voting booth because in America, that was something I was allowed—even encouraged—to do.

The last time my mother and I fought over Trump was last weekend. We were in an empty Walmart parking lot waiting for our grocery pickup, and I was asking her what she thought about Trump's latest press briefing. He had insinuated that ingesting disinfectants could potentially cure patients of coronavirus. He retracted his statement the next day, but not before thirty people in New York alone had called the poison control center because of exposure to Lysol and bleach.[11]

"Some people are just dumb, and everyone makes mistakes," my mom rushed to Trump's defense.

"Okay, sure, but that kind of mistake kills people. And it's a ridiculous and unacceptable mistake to be making as president of the United States."

"He said he was being sarcastic," my mom shrugged.

I needed a new strategy. "Do you think Trump is a good person?"

"I don't see why that matters if he is or isn't."

"Excuse me?"

"We're talking about whether he's fit for office, not whether he is a good or bad person."

"And those are separate?"

"Of course they are. The thing is, Amy, no one is a good person. We're all evil, selfish, and greedy animals by nature."

"That's not what Jesus thinks."

"Amy, stop it. You're being ridiculous."

"No, I'm not. You're the one—"

"Hello, Jessica! Thanks for shopping with Walmart today." A young Hispanic man in a light blue mask and ripped jeans

---

11   Jason Slotkin, "NYC Poison Control Sees Uptick In Calls After Trump's Disinfectant Comments," NPR, April 25, 2020.

interrupted us to say that all our groceries had already been loaded in the back.

My mom whipped around in her seat, pulling out a white envelope from the cup holder as she rolled down the window. "Thank you for your service!" she said, reaching her arm out to him.

The man laughed. "Thank you, ma'am, but it's okay."

"Are you sure? I brought it for you!"

"Yes, but I appreciate it though."

My mom nodded, and he waved as we drove away.

"What was that?" I demanded.

"I saw some woman handing a grocery helper a tip last week. I thought that was very nice, so I wanted to give our helper one, too. They're risking their lives for us, you know. I feel bad. We're lucky to have a home and jobs and food to eat. Very lucky."

And just like that, my anger vanished. We drove the rest of the way home in silence. I leaned back in my seat with my arms folded and put my feet on the dashboard. With Chinese pop music playing on the radio and the windows still rolled down, I thought about how much there was to admire and love about my mom, and how much I hated politics for getting in the way.

In 2016, John Oliver exclaimed on national TV that Donald Trump had become "America's back mole": "It may have seemed harmless a year ago, but now that it's gotten frighteningly bigger, it is no longer wise to ignore it."[12]

---

12   Melissa Locker, "John Oliver Takes on Donald Trump on *Last Week Tonight*," *Time*, February 29, 2016.

Now that four years have passed, everyone knows who Trump is: a force to be reckoned with, for better or for worse. So are his supporters. They are out in the open now, the proud half-face of the country, relieved to finally have a strong voice to believe in, to stand up and fight for.

Seeing all these supporters in the flesh makes me realize that not all of them are as ugly as I once made them out to be. Increasingly, I find myself believing that many of these supporters are normal people. Even what some would call "good" people. A quick Internet search before the 2020 elections brings up the following archetypes: a retired Air Force chief master sergeant, a mother who voted for Barack Obama in 2008, an artist and father of four, a highly educated attorney in the suburbs of Washington, DC ... The list goes on.

As a native Houstonian, I need simply to look outside my living room window to see Trump supporters sunbathing on lawns near me. I consider many of these neighbors to be good people. They are the beefy, gruff-bearded men who drove pickup trucks around town to evacuate families from their flooded homes during Hurricane Harvey. They are the picket fence families who hold open barbecues during the summer, handing out half-pound burgers and canned pears to anyone who stops by. They are the fresh-off-the-boat immigrants who chat with me in their Chinese and Vietnamese restaurants, the high school classmates I still see once a year, the family friends who invite us to their home each year to celebrate the holidays.

They are also my mother: a living emblem of the American Dream and the most thoughtful person I know. She is the person who donates to the Houston Food Bank, Texas Children's Hospital, and Operation Smile each year, the person who prepares five-dollar bills in her cupholder each morning in case she runs into panhandlers and can "pay her luck forward." She is the person who lets the children and the elderly go first, the person who wipes down restaurant tables after eating because "one should never leave a place messier than one found it," the person who always tips more than 20 percent of the bill.

"I know what it is like to work that hard," she says whenever anyone asks where the extra change went.

Of course, when I look at my mother, the first thing I see is neither a dream nor a political symbol. Instead, I see the crow's feet around her eyes and the sunspots on her hands. I hear her high-pitched laughter when she asks me, for the hundredth time, to re-explain the difference between "detective" and "dictator," and which one applies to Sherlock Holmes or Xi Jinping. I smell the worn cotton of her clothes and taste the spice in her peppercorn pancakes and mapo tofu. In everything she does, I feel the love of someone who sacrificed everything back home to give me my home here.

It is only occasionally that I see my mother as something else: the exceptional immigrant, the Chinese fugitive, the grudge-holding activist who voted for Trump out of hatred for someone across the sea.

It is only during times like this—when the political gets personal—that I see someone I love being led astray by a war-mongering loudmouth. Yet I know my mom is choosing this crowd willingly, that no matter what I say, my opinions will never outdo her lived experience. To have the freedom of choice, to be able to be a loudmouth herself—this is all she ever wanted. I would be a fool to snatch her dreams away.

When I see my mother with this MAGA hat-wearing, flag-toting, American exceptionalism-touting crowd, I cannot say I do not feel uneasy.

But when I see my mother, a proud American citizen, exercising all the freedoms she ever wanted, happy to have her family here as well as her home, I cannot help but feel happy for her, too.

MY FAVORITE
LOVE SONGS

If I had been honest in the second grade, instead of telling everyone I wanted to be an artist when I grew up, I would have said I wanted to be "married to Reese Costis."

Excluding the cartoon character Danny Phantom, Reese was the most attractive person I had ever laid eyes on. He had dark brown hair, tan skin the color of golden graham crackers, and a cute gap-toothed smile that should have been in dental commercials. Like me, he got straight As. He was also a kickball star, which was, at the time, the determinant of social status for seven- and eight-year-olds.

I was neither cute nor athletic and was twice Reese's size in both weight and emotional sensitivity, but for a while, I thought our shared zeal for academic perfection might make us more than friends. That was before Reese gave me my first nickname: "grammar Nazi." The fact he thought I was more smartass than smart hurt me, but it was the kind of hurt that made me realize how much he mattered.

From second to fifth grade, Reese was my role model, my personal trainer for how to be cool. When he started playing Yu-Gi-Oh! at the lunch table, I pretended to care about it.

When he brought Lunchables and Gushers on Menil Collection field trips, I started asking my parents for something "whiter" than shredded pork and bean curd boxes. When he chose me last for kickball because I was "too slow," I vowed to cut down my sixteen-minute mile time at the next physical exam.

My period of unrequited love for Reese coincided with my discovery of Kanye West and all the other R&B and hip-hop artists on the radio. Every morning when my mom drove my sister and me to school, I set the station to Sunny 99.1 or 104.1 KRBE and listened to Kanye pour his auto-tuned soul out in the lyrics of "Heartless," where the heavy bass, deep voice, and pensive rhythm of his songs reverberated deep in my soul. I hummed the lyrics down Chimney Rock Road and into class each week before sitting as close as I could to Reese.

I like to think it was all a coincidence that I ended up associating Reese with this song. I moved to a private school for sixth grade and never saw him again, but we said goodbye as friends. Still, whenever "Heartless" comes on in a TJMaxx or Ross, I can't help but think of the days I cried listening to T.I., Lil Wayne, and Kanye on my blue iPod shuffle as I worked on my mile time and my confidence.

The summer before seventh grade, I met Sean, an athletic Japanese boy with frizzy hair and dry humor. My parents had placed me in chemistry class with him for God knows what reason, but by the second week, I was happy to learn about Thomson and Rutherford if it meant learning more about Sean, too. Because I sat next to him every day, I quickly learned that Sean was terrible at chemistry. Yet despite how little he cared for learning, I still wanted him to be my lab partner in crime.

As far as childhood crushes went, Sean was the kind to make life feel like a teen pop song—the kind that encourages summer flings and unauthorized nights out, that always features a party that goes too far and too long but somehow stays crowded until the very end.

I am reminded of Sean every time I listen to "Tonight Tonight" by Hot Chelle Rae. As far as pop songs went in the 2010s, "Tonight Tonight" was the industry standard: repetitive, romantic, irreverent. It played on Hot 95.7 every afternoon as my mom drove me down the billboard-studded stretch of I-10, and as I shouted the lyrics out loud, I fantasized about my afternoon with Sean. Time was infinite between three o'clock in the afternoon and five. In my mind, our chemistry classroom was the party, Sean was the crowd, and I was the star, the beauty, the hopeless romantic who dreamt of love but was terrified by everything pop songs made it out to be.

On the last day of class, Sean took off his ankle bracelet and gave it to me after I asked for a memento to remember him by. After years of wear, it had turned into a rather ragged piece of string that smelled like locker room sweat.

"It's all I have," he said with a cool shrug.

"Thanks," I said, tying it onto my backpack. We walked out of the building together. The sun was just beginning to set beneath an expanse of looping freeways and violet clouds when my mom's Chevy pulled into the parking lot. I gave Sean a hug and walked away. I waved to him from the backseat of the car, figuring he was too far away to hear me shout goodbye. The party ended then, and I made my way back home.

In eighth grade, Michael put a pause on pop and introduced me to the serious intellectualism of classical music. Within the hand-chiseled walls of an elite Houston private school, we enjoyed lunch dates that consisted of *Certamen* (the Latin version of quiz bowl) and chess games. After school, they continued over Google Hangouts and under the watch of Roberto Cacciapaglia, Ólafur Arnalds, and Ludovico Einauldi—the three contemporary connoisseurs of classical elegance. With "Oceano" and "Nuvole di luce" unfolding in cathartic crescendos, we would chat about *Atlas Shrugged* and Nietzsche, and I would pretend I had read them.

As thirteen-year-olds still voice-cracking our way through puberty, Michael and I tried hard to signal our maturity. We were grown-ups in our preferences for classical music and obscure texts, and because no one bothered to stop our daydreaming (or cared to), our efforts at self-delusion succeeded.

For all of our mature talks, however, our brief stint at romance was the opposite. In the two months we dated, we called each other "munchkins." We never kissed. We did hold hands, but never for long—neither of us wanted to bring up the sweat that collected between our palms. The boldest thing I ever did was sit on his lap for a holiday party photo op, but even that somehow felt wrong. We broke up after convincing ourselves that mental intimacy did not belong in the physical realm.

Looking back, I admit now that no amount of classical music could have concealed the fact that, as with all of middle school, we lived in a time not for growing old, but for growing up. The Christmas present Michael got me eight years ago—a comic book of Calvin and Hobbes—always reminds me of that.

I met Ethan the summer before high school, a time when I began entertaining thoughts about a career and long-term relationships. We both attended a three-week summer program called The Center for Talented Youth at Johns Hopkins University, and by the end of the program, we liked each other terribly.

I wish we had met at the Friday night dance where, after a week of classes and activities, all the campers crowded into the gym for a night of administration-endorsed fist pumping. Without a date to distract me, the whole thing felt like middle school homecomings all over again: over-dressed teachers drinking punch on the sides, girls looking nervous in strapless dresses and braces, and Billboard Hot 100 songs playing with all the cuss words poorly bleeped out, which of course only made everyone scream them louder. The night passed with mosh pits and virgin mojitos until the last song came on, which, according to CTY tradition, was always "American Pie" by Don McLean, a 1970s folk-rock song about the plane crash that killed Buddy Holly, among others, and how everyone just wanted to return to the good ole days, drinking and dancing and singing all their sorrows away.

That first Friday, I learned that CTYers had their own dance for this song. We started in a ring around the gym, swaying together until the rock-and-roll chorus crashed in. As the tempo quickened and the volume rose, the ring broke and we all ran to the center of the floor, jumping like sardines being shaken in a can, hollering goodbye to some sweet Miss American Pie at the top of our lungs.

Ethan and I met the second week, and at the third dance, we held hands from start to finish of our last American Pie. When the song ended, the two of us left the building and sat alone on the courtyard lawn, watching fireflies dance in the grass and humming a chorus ringing of goodbyes.

I boarded my plane the next day with a letter from Ethan and "American Pie" still ringing in my head. I set it on repeat on my phone and dozed off. When I woke up three hours later to the thud and an announcement that we had landed in Houston, Don McLean was still crooning in my ear, saying something about two people in love, dancing.

Ethan and I saw each other again in New York years later. He was there for a job interview, I was there for school, and we celebrated our unlikely reunion on a rainy Sunday afternoon over chocolate chip pancakes and truffle pizza at Carroll Place. I asked him how he was doing; he asked me the same. We spent the rest of our meal reminiscing about our CTY days, both of us knowing but neither of us acknowledging that after so many years, American Pie had turned bittersweet.

Michael Number Two and I met the following summer at another camp. I had my first kiss with him.

We were sitting on the steps of Butler Library at Columbia University when he put his hand on my lap and turned to me with that look in his eyes. *Fuck it*, I thought, *why not. I'll never see him again if this sucks.*

"I've never kissed anyone before, so if you want this to happen," I said, gesturing back and forth at the two of us, "you're going to have to teach me how."

My terms and conditions should also have specified that all I wanted was a little lip-to-lip action. Instead, I received a full-blown lesson on The French Kiss.

"How was that?" he asked after our spit exchange was over.

"Mmm—mhm," I forced, wondering how to spit out a wad of his saliva without offending him and also why on earth, if Columbia had chandeliers in the dining halls and sprinklers that went off in the middle of the day, it did not also have emergency paper towel stands outside.

Some songs we listen to for the music, and others, for the people and places they remind us of. For those three weeks of summer, I had my alarm clock set to "Classic" by MKTO, a pop song about reliving classic moments, in the hopes that it would one day remind me of how New York first took my breath away. Never did I expect to look back at a literal interpretation of this.

A few months after Michael taught me how to kiss, my best friend at the time, Chris, taught me what it meant to be friends with benefits. I stopped listening to "Classic" after that. The verse mentioned something about getting it on with Michael and Prince, but for years, I misheard the lyrics as "Michael" and "Chris."

Gabe was the first boy I dated for over a year and the first boy I seriously considered marrying. To ask me to senior prom, Gabe popped out of a handmade cardboard cake holding an actual cake in his hands. "PROM?" the cardboard cake read in glittering pink letters. At the time, I had wanted to climb into that cake myself and pop out with a ring.

That year, Gabe and I were Southern lovebirds in both a real and make-believe world. We danced at prom and on stage, in our high school's rendition of the 1943 musical "Oklahoma!" In both places, we were a couple who made one another feel like home. Our trope as singing Southern lovebirds was not an act; it was more like a happy cliché, and the truth.

When college came around, we drew the curtains on our own show. He decided to attend Yale University, I decided to attend NYU, and because neither of us wanted to be so far from home for the next four years, we decided to say goodbye. Of course, we could not help texting every week and calling, too, but when he came to visit me the following spring, I sat in the hallway crying on the night I told him I had moved on.

That year, in trying not to think about Gabe and my nauseating doubts about leaving him, I ended up not thinking at all. I was a college kid in New York City and decided to act the part, doing the kinds of things that were excusable only because every other eighteen-year-old kid in the city was doing them too. I got a couple fake IDs. I clubbed. I discovered vodka and tequila and weed. I got high for the first time on an East Village rooftop and fell for a boy who introduced me to "Canna Butta Kisses"—an Elli Ingram song about drugs and cigarettes—and confessed his love for me. But unlike the alcohol and the weed, the sex we had later was a mistake.

———————————

Another mistake I made in college was saying yes to a boy I did not like enough. I feel sorry for Phil, the tall, courteous fencer who asked me out only to discover a year later that I had been in a passionate love affair with my eating disorder the entire time we hung out. During the months we saw each other, I heard only the voice inside my head. If Phil and I had a song, I no longer remember it.

———————————

After Phil, I took time off college in the spring to regain my weight and my self-esteem. I returned to New York the following fall. Overeager for companionship and overflowing with estrogen, I signed up for the club leaders' orientation summit and there, in the last session of the day, I met Michael Number Three.

Michael Number Three turned out to be a half-Polish, half-Taiwanese genius with eclectic interests and a dorky grin. He was a walking resume: an impressive and intimidating presence, perfect on paper. Over dinner, he told me about his full-time tech fellowship in Silicon Valley, his love for French culinary techniques, and his interest in plays, musicals, and me.

He waited until the check came to tell me about his girlfriend.

"I plan on breaking up with her soon," he clarified.

The insinuation was subtle but clear, so I waited. Eventually, we started dating, and only then did I realize I should have waited longer, until he had told me about everything else. Like the poker addiction. The insomnia. The fact that he found most people in the world incredibly stupid, and that he hated stupid people.

"Sometimes I hate myself, too," he told me one winter night as we walked along Chelsea Piers.

"I'm so sorry, Michael."

"It's okay. I'll be okay. Gambling is a good distraction. So are you—shit, I didn't mean it that way. All I'm trying to say is that you don't have to worry. I haven't thought about suicide since high school."

Michael and I spent many evenings cooking dinner together at his small walk-up apartment in the East Village. Sometimes while we cooked, Michael would walk over to his speakers and put ZHU on blast from the living room, filling the air with house and electronic synthesizer beats.

As the water boiled, my mind would too, drifting along with ZHU's mad, moody drives. I thought about Michael's depression. I thought about the friendships I had lost over his ex, and about the rumor that she was now an alcoholic because of me. I thought about the relationship I wanted to have and the one I did. I thought about the fact that I was not as happy as I wanted to be, and that no musical or Michelin-grade meal could belie this reality. Some nights as we cooked, I felt like the meat oozing myoglobin in his sous vide. I was sure Michael could see the stress bleeding right out of me, that ZHU's eerie falsettos and distorted snares were taunting me.

The ZHU song that Michael played for us most often was "Chasing Marrakech." A mix of soft organ chords, a pounding bassline, and repetitive snares, the song told of telling lies and running away to Marrakech, the former imperial city of western Morocco.

I ran away the night I finally told Michael I was unhappy. "It's not you, it's me," I said before leaving his apartment. As I closed the door behind me, I realized ZHU, not Michael, had been the genius all along. I was not in love with my boyfriend; I was in love with the lies I told myself about him. If Michael was perfect on paper, it was because I had tucked all the red flags between the lines.

"I'll miss you," I said before running off to Peru the next week. I couldn't tell if that was a lie or not, but I tried not to think too hard about it. Spring break had arrived. I had packed light. With so little baggage, everything was supposed to feel easy. I stepped out onto the beaches of Lima and breathed.

Now, my favorite love songs span almost every genre I know. For a while after my breakup, I sang them for myself. Then I met my current boyfriend, Peter, who is a remix of everyone who came before. He is pop when he dances and blues when he cries openly. He is country when he goes horseback riding and jazz when he hands me chocolate roses on an ordinary Wednesday afternoon. He is folk when we browse Brooklyn markets for Italian ingredients and classical when he holds his jacket over my head to block the midnight rain.

If Peter is the last boy I like, he will have a hundred songs to his name one day. So far, they include "Your Man" by Josh Turner, "The Hill of Yearning" by April 2nd, "Get Right Witcha" by Migos, "Miss You" by Cashmere Cat, and the acoustic version of "Intentions" by Justin Bieber. Like all songs, they are time capsules of memory. They are meaningful to me in a way that is meaningless to others. Of course, they were meaningless to us too, until they weren't.

Six years ago—three before I met Peter—I started keeping a playlist of every song I have ever loved. With 3,780 songs, it encapsulates every feeling I have ever known. I like to think that, if not for my past crushes, I may never have known them.

Peter could be the last boy I love. But if he is not, the jukebox will keep running, the songs will keep shuffling, and the people will keep coming as new music in my life. As with new songs, I will not know how to feel about them until the end.

IT TAKES A VILLAGE

Nothing I did in New York prepared me for my week in a Ghanaian village.

I believe my NYU professors had the best of intentions in recruiting Stern International Volunteers to "promote sustainable economic development and educational empowerment" in the village of Woadze Tsatoe.[13] But as a privileged undergraduate business student, the last thing I wanted when I signed up for a social entrepreneurship course in Ghana was to come back a self-righteous voluntourist. You know the kind—the private schoolers who teach English in Costa Rica to buff up their college resumes; the backpackers who fly to Thailand for nondescript "community development" projects in exchange for day trips; the blond-haired, blue-eyed caricatures who "do good" in Kenya and come back with an Instagram feed full of smiling dark-skinned children.[14]

I signed up to become an international volunteer to see what all the hubbub was about. My curiosity was driven primarily by cynicism and ego: if voluntourism really were a

---

13   "SIV: Social Entrepreneurship in Ghana," Stern Around the World, New York University Stern School of Business, accessed August 15, 2020.

14   Brittany Edwardes, "Short Term Volunteer Abroad Programs & Mission Trips (1 Week & 2 Weeks)," Volunteer Forever, February 11, 2020.

sham, I wanted to experience it for myself. This was how I, a privileged, middle-class, eighteen-year-old freshman in college, ended up in a spring semester course that, almost like a brochure, promised to "combine theory with hands-on implementation and cultural immersion."[15] I spent every Wednesday morning creating business plans, drafting education lessons, and calling with Robert Tornu, our village guide and local director of the nonprofit Adanu, but as the weeks passed by, I worried that all I was really doing was planning my own "unforgettable experience" in someone else's life.

By the time spring break rolled around, I was in a complete panic. The irony was not lost on me that, like many voluntourists I had previously mocked, I might be spending my time in Ghana doing the same things. I buried my distress in self-denial. Surely, ninety pages of English lessons, fifty spare computer parts, four hundred children's books, and twenty Excel spreadsheets full of financial statements and accounting lessons would be enough to set ourselves apart from the voluntourists I so despised.

On the day of the flight, I boarded the plane almost convinced that my week would truly be beneficial for the villagers I would meet. And then my classmates and I arrived in Accra, spending two nights in the city before driving via charter bus to Woadtze Tsatoe.

Woadtze Tsatoe is a bucolic little village buried deep in the Volta region in sub-Saharan Africa where the papayas are sweeter than syrup and the air shimmers with heat. Though

---

15   "SIV: Social Entrepreneurship in Ghana."

it is hidden in the thicketed mountainside, the land itself is quite flat and arid. Clay huts, metal-sheathed sheds, and African mahogany trees dot the landscape. Yellow flowers bloom in the fields, and sand the color of hazelwood bark borders a river teeming with silver freshwater fish, which are caught and smoked each day. In the center of the village stands a plain, yam-colored building with open windows and dark green chalkboards, which serves both as a meeting place for the village elders and a primary school for the children.

I spent my mornings here teaching school children and my afternoons discussing marketing principles with the women and elders who ran the village economy. In return, they taught me about their lives, about gratitude, and about relative happiness, and I watched and learned. Each day was a new lesson in reality: I learned how patterned sponge blocks are pressed and dyed into white cloth. I learned how concrete is made from mixing gravel, sand, and cement with water. I learned about the lake where the water comes from, and how to carry it in a shallow metal basin on my head. I learned about the hollow *shekere* gourds and goatskin *djembe* drums and how to dance to their jubilant polyrhythms. Mostly, I learned that life here was lived with a profound simplicity. It was honest, direct, unadulterated by the blue funk of industrial life. When I realized that life here was making me reconsider how I wanted to live my own, I realized just how different real change could be from any theory proposed in the air-conditioned classrooms of downtown New York City.

What started as a desire to help others soon turned into a desire to hide my own embarrassment. With the Ghanaian sun as my own personal sauna, I found myself unable to urinate for two days. It was not that I did not want to; in fact, I drank a bottle of water about every half-hour in between solving addition problems with second graders and teaching profit-loss statements to the businesswomen. But because every bottle of water I drank left my body minutes later as sweat, it was not until the third day that I asked to use the restroom, after which I was directed to the nearest clay hut housing two cavernous holes in the ground.

My own stench hit me next. As it turns out, antiperspirant and deodorant do not work in Ghana in March, when the country's dry heat turns your entire body into a leaking fire hydrant. As I lifted my arms to balance a shallow metal basin of water on my head for the wet cement mix, I became acutely aware of the fact that the villagers did not just have to deal with my ineptitude as a construction worker; they also had to deal with my BO.

The third thing that hit me, in addition to the heat and the stench, was just how much of a stranger I could be. In this small village six hours away from the capital city of Accra, no one saw me as the straight-A undergraduate studying Sustainable Business at NYU and working a Teach For America internship down on Wall Street. Here, I was an unfit outsider. A privileged visitor in a stranger's home. As I wiped away the sweat trickling down my legs and squatted in the shade, I did not feel like an international social worker here to create value for people in poverty. I felt more like a toad baking alive, croaking a song about changing the world without knowing what it looked like.

One day, the villagers asked us to make a trip to the market. With the sky still a soft and sleepy lavender, Robert drove us from the village to an endless maze of open-air stalls offering everything from live chickens to replica soccer jerseys. Stall owners were buzzing about; the market was already crowded. On the bus, Robert split us up into pairs. He handed each pair a list of ingredients and twenty-five cedis (about four dollars) before clearing his throat into a microphone.

"NYU bee-suh-ness students!" he began in his deep, booming voice. "Here you see our informal eh-conomy in ak-shun. Go use deh bee-suh-ness skills to get deh best price for deh vee-llagers! Go, go!"

When we did not move off the bus, he frowned and clarified his message.

"Deh vee-llage wee-men gave me dese lists and told me dey were for you. Your job is to bargain for deh next meal. Good luck! You have thuh-ty mee-nuts!"

So for the next hour, we stumbled from stall to stall bargaining for raw chicken thighs, red peppers the size and shape of marbles, cassava dough, and other items we did not recognize in a language we could not understand. It was a far cry from what my classmates thought we would be doing that morning: teaching children the names of everyday items in English.

I squeezed past buckets of live fish, hand soap, and sacks of various colored grains before coming across a stall with red peppers. I nudged my friend Chloe, cleared my throat loudly enough so the stall owner could hear, and pointed at them.

"Five cedis," the stall owner said. I heard Robert's voice in my head telling me it was acceptable to bargain at the market.

"Three?" I squeaked. A chorus of laughter rippled from nearby stalls.

"No, no, no," she shook her head, trying hard not to laugh herself. "Cannot. Five."

"I, uh, hmm." I turned to Chloe for help, but she looked as frazzled as I did.

"Oooee!" the women around us giggled with glee. They began shouting to one another through their batik cloth dividers, chattering about what I could only guess was our audacity to bargain and our inability to speak in Ewe. The owner clicked her tongue and adjusted her pink head wrap.

"Okay. Four," she said. She took the cedis from my hand before I could say anything else and counted out her money. She handed the change back along with a small bag of peppers before waving me away, amusement dancing on her face.

"Akpe na wò," I managed as I shuffled past. Her eyes grew wide, and another crest of laughter broke from the neighboring stalls.

"Akpe na wò, akpe na wò!" the stall owners called out after us, happy to know that, though we were incompetent foreigners, we at least knew their words for "thank you."

The longer Chloe and I wandered around the market, the less intimidated we felt. I knew the women were intentionally giving me higher prices to see how far my stammering could go, but soon I began playing along—the more entertainment I provided, the lower the price dropped.

That afternoon, I carried five bags of ingredients back to the villagers, feeling humbled but accomplished. School had already ended, and work was gradually being replaced by laughing, singing, and dancing under a rectangular grass awning. The children were running in the fields, the village elders were resting in plastic chairs, and two young men sat under the trees, weaving kente cloth with black, red, green, and gold threads. A woman stood nearby skinning, gutting, and smoking fish over a large grilling pit.

"Wow," one of the schoolteachers said when he saw us toting our groceries. "Good job."

"You did well," said another young man with him.

"Good bargain?" a woman asked.

We all smiled and nodded.

She smiled back as a few women snorted. They each gave us a validating thumbs-up.

Robert then began parading us around the village as if we had done everyone a great service.

"Dey are proud of you, espe-shully deh wee-men. Everyting dat dey needed, you got!" As he took us around the families' wooden and clay huts, he explained to us that in this village, it was the women, not the men, who took care of all financial and economic matters.

"Dat is why you see only wee-men selling at deh marketplace and talking bee-suh-ness tings here. Deh men do all deh physical work, you know, feesh-ing, plowing, building."

"Imagine if every American business was run only by women," a classmate whispered next to me.

"I can't," I muttered back.

Later that night, I thought about my two days of "social entrepreneurship" over a dinner of fried chicken *jollof*, *gari fortor*, beef and vegetable stew, rice and corn cakes, and ripe papaya. As I ate, I thought about my intentions for being here, about voluntourism, and about how I felt less like a Western do-gooder than a wide-eyed child. At worst, I was a nuisance. At best, a joke. Who was really helping whom? Who was teaching and being taught? Before falling asleep that night, I wrote one line in my journal:

"The women could have gotten everything they needed from the market today using only half the money we did."

The rest of the week only amplified the questions I had about my role and purpose here. I tried to stick to the script of a well-read volunteer, but it was always in the most unexpected moments that I felt the change I had wanted to see.

On the third day of teaching, I grew frustrated with the fact that half of my students were playing with eraser stubs and the other half were half asleep at their desk. Desperate to dispel the boredom in the room, I asked everyone to come outside into the field with me, where I spent the rest of the morning teaching them Simon Says and the chant to "Heads, Shoulders, Knees, and Toes." By lunchtime, they had learned more English in the past hour than in the past two days.

At lunch, the creative head of batik production, Vida, came up to us to show us her new products.

"New bags and purses, what you think?" she asked, holding up a zippered pouch with violet patterns that looked like palm leaves.

"That would be perfect for an Etsy store," my friend Caitlyn exclaimed.

"So would backpacks and laptop bags. My friends would love those," James added.

"I'll set up a website as soon as we get home."

"Vida, would you let us teach you how to sell things online? All you need to give us is a name, a logo, and a story."

And from that one conversation, Amenuveve Batik was born. Its name came from the Ewe word for "grace," its logo was a West African Adinkra symbol representing collaboration toward a greater good, and its story was ours: an odd assortment of college students from New York City working with female artisans from the Afadzato South District of Ghana.

On the fourth day, Mr. Bright, the second grade teacher, walked by while I was painting ladybugs on the side of the school and asked how college in America worked.

"Do you think I have chance of getting in one day? I want to study plants and biology. Can I come vee-sit you?" he asked, looking away.

I put down my brush, and the two of us talked about college until the red sun began to sink. When the bus came to pick us up, only half of us left for our designated lodge. The rest of us stayed to cook dinner with our host families and spend the night.

Once we had gathered under the grass-thatched awning, Robert began pairing us off one by one with our hosts. I met my host mother last. She sat at the back of the crowd, wearing a sunflower yellow head wrap and a blue striped dress. When she came to greet me, I noticed she had two faded tattoo marks below her eyes like thin, dark arrowheads. She spoke no English. She simply smoothed out my messy hair and pulled me into a tight hug. Then she cupped my face in both hands, studying me as if I were a ceramic relief, before leading me to her hut, arm in arm.

Two young children, a boy and a girl, were playing outside when we arrived. She signaled for me to sit with them before ducking under an entryway. The children climbed into my lap, touching my face and giggling until she returned, carrying with her all the ingredients I had purchased from the market two days ago: okra, cassava pulp, smoked fish, green peppers and baby tomatoes, and a red sachet of chili powder for seasoning. She held them up and motioned to the four of us. *We will eat together,* her gestures read. I nodded and stood up to help her prepare the fire, but she whistled through her teeth and shook her head. I was to stay seated until dinner was ready.

So as the sun drooped beneath the trees, I watched my host mother make okra stew in a large pot over the fire. Like a quilt, nightfall fell quickly and silently over us, and soon we could only see each other through the lick of flames.

With a white ladle, my host mother poured out a bowl for me, herself, and her children. She passed around warm cassava cakes. We dipped the cakes into the soup like bread and sank our teeth in. My mouth filled with the spice of the okra, the sweetness of the peppers, and the saltiness of the fish. It tasted like a joyous dance.

We had no words for each other, but we spent dinner laughing and smiling until my cheeks hurt. Our arms touched as we ate. Her children alternated between clinging onto her and sitting on top of me.

Near the end of the meal, my host mother pointed at some okra in my bowl.

"Fetri," she said.

"Feh-tree?"

"Fetri!" She nodded her head excitedly and grinned.

I laughed and, pointing again to the okra, said, "Okra."

"Oh-kah-rah."

"Yes!"

Then she pointed to the pot. "Detsi."

"Detsi. Stew," I said back.

Then she pointed at the smoked fish, the cassava cakes, and the peppers. She pointed at the bowls we were using, the white ladle, the pot over a bed of diminishing flames. She pointed at the earth we sat on, the yellow moon, the rising stars, and my eyes. She pointed at her daughter and called out a name. She did the same with her son. Then she pointed at me.

"Amy," I said.

"Aye-mee." The syllables floated off her tongue like dandelion fluff. She pointed at herself and said, "Akutor."

"Ah-koo-tor." She smiled and reached over to squeeze my hand.

We kept our language game going until Robert called out for us.

"Meeting, everyone, meeting at deh lake!" It was too dark to find my way, but Akutor led me by hand until we were standing on a sandy shore where the other host families sat in a ring of plastic chairs around a blazing bonfire. Akutor and I sat together as Robert told us—first in Ewe and then in English—the stories of the clever spider who fooled the gods, the riddles of the snake and the elephant, and the history of how the Volta people came to be. Following the folklore came the music. Young men sat in a loose semicircle with their *djembe, dunun, ashiko,* and *shekere,* and the women began whooping and clapping in their seats. Akutor was the first to stand up and start dancing. Her shadows danced with her underneath the flames. She held out her hands and called to me, "Amy, Amy, Amy!"

As the inky sky turned grey with smoke, the two of us swayed together, face to face, our elbows bent at our sides and our feet stomping in the ground. I followed her lead. Sparks flew. Others joined. We danced until the earth felt like quicksand.

Sometime later, my host mother walked me back to her home and motioned toward the back of the room, where a quilt and a mosquito net had been laid out for me.

"Akpe na wò," I whispered as she slipped away. I fell asleep in a pool of sweat, bone-weary and content.

We said our goodbyes the following afternoon. It was our last day in the village, and as the volunteers and villagers shook hands, we promised to see other again one day. I ran from Mr. Bright's second grade classroom with a sheet of construction paper asking everyone to sign it. Akutor did not know how to write her name, so she drew a messy scribble across the page. I made sure she signed my note last; I wanted her to hold me until I had to leave. As everyone else headed toward the bus, I lingered behind. Akutor kissed me on the cheek, and I burst into tears, whispering "akpe na wò, akpe na wò, akpe na wò" to my host mother over and over again, grateful the only words I knew in Ewe were the ones I wanted to express then.

On the flight home, I thought about the part of the world that was inhabited by street vendors selling fresh coconuts for two cedis each and businesswomen balancing crates of baguettes, plantain chips, milk cartons, fresh fruits, nuts, and Adinkra pastries on their heads. I thought of the canoes that set out to catch fish before the sun rose and the bonfires and tall tales that flared up after the sun set. I thought of Mr. Bright, of Robert, of Akutor and her two children, and I wondered how much of me they would remember, and how much of them I would never forget.

As a Stern International Volunteer, I had come to Woadtze Tsatoe bearing suitcases full of what I thought were gifts: computers, books, lesson plans, me. A week later, I was not so sure what any of that was. Yes, they were objective improvements in terms of business acumen and physical goods, but by the time I left, I wondered who the richer party really was.

I landed at LaGuardia Airport tired and hungry. I called a taxi back to my dormitory on Fifth Avenue and texted my friend John that, if he had not yet eaten, I would love to catch up with him over a late dinner. He was standing outside when I arrived. Together, we walked down University Place into Ramen Takumi. We sat down at a corner table. I told John to order whatever he wanted for me before excusing myself to the restroom.

It had been only a week since I had my own private restroom, but never had a white toilet seat looked so inviting. The sound of a flushing toilet gave me goosebumps. The sink was small and covered in soap scabs, but its faucet emitted clean, running water from pipes I could not see. I ran my hands in the water for what seemed like an eternity. I cupped some in my hands and drank it. I had taken for granted that in New York, tap water was water I could drink.

I stood there watching the faucet run, imagining Akutor's eyes widen as I showed her how it worked. I wanted her to have a restroom like this that was all her own. I wanted her to taste how sweet New York tap water was. I wanted her to try gyoza and shoyu ramen at an air-conditioned izakaya, and I wanted her to listen to American pop songs and classical music as she ate. After that, I wanted to take her back to my dormitory on Fifth Avenue. I wanted to sneak her onto the seventeenth floor rooftop and show her that the lights twinkling across the East River were breathtaking, like stars in the Ghanaian night, except across the sea.

Embarrassment replaced excitement then. As did guilt. Right after praising Akutor's home, I had imagined replacing it with mine. I thought back to my initial objective for the trip: avoid voluntourism at all costs. Standing here, realizing just how much I missed my privileges as a middle-class American, how easily I reverted to worshipping nonessential comforts, I realized I had set myself up for failure. There was no way I could have gone to Ghana—or anywhere—as a foreign volunteer and pretend that tourism was not at the core of the experience.

And that was what it was: a temporary experience. Visiting Woadze Tsatoe made me realize it did not need volunteers to thrive. Akutor and the rest of the villagers lived their lives just fine without us. They may have enjoyed our presence and our willingness to help for a while, but I am not so sure they would have wanted it forever.

Even as I write this, I wonder if they are doing better now, without any more of my meddling.

MAHJONG IN THE AFTERNOONS

———

When I was eight, my grandparents flew from Beijing to Houston to spend six months with my family. During those months, life felt like one extended summer vacation. The two of them arrived at the airport lugging one suitcase of essentials and two suitcases of toys, games, and clothes for my sister and me. On weekdays, I rushed through homework so that my grandparents and I could play Chinese checkers and card games until my mom dragged me to bed. On weekends, we played games for as long as I could stay awake.

My grandparents owned their own set of mahjong tiles wrapped in a crimson leather jacket. I loved the heavy sound it made when they placed the set on the kitchen table and unclasped the lock. Inside the jacket lay 144 jade and white tiles, two dice, and hours to be gambled away.

"This is a difficult game," my grandpa announced in Mandarin during my first lesson. "We will teach you how to master the art."

"The art of gambling," my grandma corrected.

"Right."

"And winning."

The tiles clattered to the table. My grandparents shuffled them and stacked them into four adjacent walls. We shook the dice and took turns drawing our tiles. Then they began teaching me about the three suits—*tiao, wan,* and *bing*—the four winds, the three dragons, how to *chi* from the right and *peng* from the left to steal others' tiles, how to form a *geng* and claim extra money for four-of-a-kind, and most importantly, how to *hu*—win.

"I remember learning this as a kid," my grandma said as she discarded her first tile. It landed with a staccato click. "My dad taught me before the Cultural Revolution days. It was the game for late nights and extended family. Of course, that was before Mao came and destroyed everything. The Red Army took my dad's business away and forced me to be a schoolteacher. I couldn't stand up to them—I was thin and short as a bean sprout, even back then. But no one messes with your grandma. I made for a clever and intimidating teacher. All the class clowns loved and feared me," my grandma giggled. My grandpa nodded his head vigorously. "I remember chucking chalk at people's foreheads if I caught them falling asleep," she continued. "I smacked kids with my ruler if I caught them picking their nose or biting their fingernails, like this." She brought the Six Barrel tile down on my grandpa's hand repeatedly to demonstrate.

"Yes, your grandma was the queen of respect. A true—" My grandpa paused between smacks. "—force."

"What do you mean, *was?*" my grandma scowled, throwing the tile into the center pot. "Your grandpa knows nothing about me. We only saw each other twice before we were married. I was twenty when he left for the army. He worked as some airplane engineer and came home practically deaf after listening to all that mechanical whirring and communist brainwashing. Not that he would have listened to me anyway."

"I'm not deaf," my grandpa protested. "And I do listen. And cook, and clean, and make breakfast, and get the groceries. And I—"

"Oh, oh, my bad. Let me rephrase. You do all the things that I did alone for years. And you're deaf unless Amy's talking." I tried to hide my laughter as he waved his hand at her.

Then my grandpa changed the subject. "I miss the years we raised you in Beijing, Amy. You were only four months old when we brought you back to live with us. I used to carry you on my back, up and down the stairs to the basement vegetable market every day," he said. "Everyone in the building knew who you were. You were our little celebrity."

"You should have seen the way your grandpa peacocked you around, thinking every compliment for you was also for him." My grandma rolled her eyes.

"You had this obsession with milk-flavored ice cream and McDonald's fries," my grandpa went on, his retrospection undeterred. "I'll never forget that time we brought you to a fancy peking duck place, but you cried so hard for fries that I had to leave you with Grandma and run to McDonald's."

"Yes, yes, your grandpa, the strong and youthful hero," my grandma mocked. "No knee pain, no diabetes, no hearing problems, no memory loss, nothing. Faster than the North Wind," she said as picked up the tile and tossed it away, "and smarter than the Small Chick." She picked up another. "Just a young, sprightly man in his prime."

My grandpa nodded seriously. "I still am."

My grandma burst out laughing.

"You both are!" I piped in. Then I stole the tile my grandpa had just discarded and asked if that was okay to do.

"Ah, how our little tiger has grown," my grandpa said, nodding.

They stopped bickering then, focusing instead on explaining the game until I finally won my first round. They brought out a few dollar bills each and stuffed them in my hand.

"Winner's pot!" my grandma explained.

"Don't tell your mom," my grandpa said. My grandma nodded, in agreement with him for the first time all afternoon.

My grandparents came again when I was ten. This time, my grandpa was in a wheelchair, and my grandma stood scowling next to him, her frame thinner than before, her hair shorter and ash white.

"Lao Lao! Lao Ye!" I called, running up to them at baggage claim. My grandpa stood up and came shuffling over to me.

"He's fine," my grandma answered before I could ask. "Your mom just made him sit on this piece of trash because she thinks he's old and useless now."

"Ma!" my mom scowled. My grandpa chuckled.

"Your grandma isn't so young anymore, either," he whispered to me.

"XUE RAY GUANG!" my grandma shouted. "If you think that's whispering, you really are deaf!"

Once we were back home, they settled in their room with their newspapers and chrysanthemum tea as we unpacked their suitcases for them. When I found the set of mahjong tiles, I pulled it out and smiled. Though my grandparents seemed to have aged physically, the mahjong proved to me that everything else was normal. They still wanted to play, to teach, to reminisce about old times.

There was one spring afternoon I remember particularly well. I was sitting between them at the table, eating the last Magnum fudge bar from the fridge. Rain was pitter-pattering against the windowsills and echoing down the chimney stack. The warm yellow glow of the kitchen light was shining a spotlight on the tiles as we poured them out.

"Xǐ pái ba!"my grandma announced. *Let's wash the tiles!*

We shuffled the pieces, turned them face down, and stacked them in four walls. My grandpa asked if I needed to hear the rules again.

"Bú yòng." *No need.* I reminded them I was almost ten years old, no longer the baby they raised or a child who forgot the rules.

We played eight games that afternoon, waiting out the rain within our jade tiled walls. I won every game but the first. I told myself that was normal: I was a fast learner, and I had both luck and a competitive spirit on my side. Confident that I would win the last game after looking at the tiles I had drawn, I decided to form the most difficult arrangement of all: *yi tiao long,* one long dragon. We had almost run out of new tiles to draw when I won, stealing my grandpa's Nine Sticks to complete the suit along with a triplet of Red Dragons and a pair of North Winds.

"Húle!" I shouted, laying down my tiles for my grandparents to see.

They peered at the tiles and grinned, looking almost relieved.

"That's double money for you!" my grandpa exclaimed cheerfully.

"Yes! Dragons earn double because they represent power, wealth, and a long life," my grandma explained.

Before I could reply, they shoved all of their remaining money into my hands.

"Don't tell your mom."

"But this is your—"

"Please. It makes us happy."

When they noticed my hesitation, my grandpa began listing reasons I should accept their gift: It was a well-deserved prize. It was money that would bring me luck and skill for the next few weeks. It was a four-month-early birthday present. It was a ten-month early *hong bao* for Chinese New Year. It was an investment in my future, and most importantly, it was money they had already decided to give away.

"Forming *yi tiao long* means you'll live a long, good life. We'd be offended if you didn't let us help get you there," my grandpa explained.

My grandma nodded, her beady eyes fixed on me. "Besides, it's almost impossible for a beginner to win with *yi tiao long* early on in their mahjong careers. We're being generous because we're proud."

Only then did I suspect my grandparents had been letting me win this whole time.

"I promise I'll pay you back tenfold!" I exclaimed as I helped put away the tiles. "When I'm older, I'll be rich!"

My grandparents chuckled. "We'll make sure we live until then."

My grandparents visited us twice more after that, once when I was eleven and once when I was thirteen. During both visits, we still played mahjong in the afternoons, but our games were no longer an exercise of pretend. In the first visit, my grandparents stopped letting me win. In the second, their jokes, once innocent and playful, turned sour and bitter with complaints. With each tile they discarded, my grandparents tossed out their pains. Green Dragon. *Diabetes.* One Barrel. *Arthritis.* Nine Sticks. *Insomnia.* East Wind. *Constipation.* North Wind. *Migraines.* Red Dragon. *Your grandpa.* White Dragon. *Lost youth.*

"Āiyā, we've gotten old," my grandpa sighed.

"No, you haven't!" I insisted. It was a lie, of course. I knew they were getting old because now, they were acting as if they'd never grown up. Their lives were like stop-motion films, with each individual frame showing me that the older they got, the more childlike, impatient, and tantrum-prone they became.

My grandma aged faster than my grandpa. Rather than acknowledge her declining memory and strength, she blamed everyone around her for her loss of control. One afternoon, the three of us were playing mahjong again, and she had just lost four games in a row.

"Looks like you're having bad luck today," my grandpa teased.

"I've had bad luck since the day I met you," she snapped back. Weary resentment creased her brow. As if a dam had burst inside her, the grievances and accusations of the past six decades came bursting from her lips. *You should have married the army, not me. You should have written me letters. You should have helped raise your kids.*

"Sixty years later, you're writing me these shitty love poems on WeChat. Where were they when I was twenty?"

My grandpa stole a tile from me and pretended not to hear.

"See, Amy, he still never listens to me. Sixty years of marriage and—"

"Āiyā. You know it's hard for me to hear. And it's not like you ever have anything good to say about me."

"Lao Lao, I think Lao Ye just wants to—"

"No no, let him finish." She turned to my grandpa then. "Anything else?"

"No."

"Well, I have something to say." She leaned forward in her chair. "I never should have married you."

For a few minutes, all we could hear were the clicking of tiles as we took turns discarding, stealing, and drawing them from the walls.

"I wish we could go back in time," my grandpa finally said. "I miss being able to run with you on my shoulders, Amy. I miss thinking about what was next."

"Nothing's next, old man. Our deaths are next. Why don't we just go now, in fact. One right after the other. It'll save everyone else a lot of trouble." My grandma snatched a tile from him to form a triplet of South Winds. "Your turn," she huffed.

My grandpa won the game with his next draw. He laughed with delight and laid out his tiles. My grandma stood up from the table and left without handing him any money.

"It's just a game!" my grandpa called after her, shaking his head.

"Go to hell."

I put away the mahjong set after that.

The leather-bound mahjong case collected dust as I went through high school. My grandparents forgot to take it back to Beijing, and without them, I no longer felt the urge to play. I called my grandparents occasionally on weekends, but soon I began dreading our conversations.

Their stop-motions had turned into a reel of health complications. One time, my grandma called from the hospital to announce she had fractured her spine from sneezing too hard. Another time, she called to confess that she had broken her wrist on her way to Carrefour, having refused my mom's suggestion to take a taxi and instead getting crushed between two men in a crowded bus. A third time, my grandma called not to talk about herself, but to tattle on my grandpa.

"He keeps eating sugar even after his diabetes clinician told him not to, and his knee arthritis is so bad he won't take his bike out to buy breakfast!"

It felt strange, hearing their world fall apart even though I once thought that was impossible. A part of me still thought it was just a fluke, a stroke of bad luck.

A motorbike accident that left my grandpa unable to walk for two weeks finally convinced us of the obvious. My mom begged them to move to Texas with us. The summer before college, I flew with her to Beijing to bring them home. We moved them into a one-story house five minutes away from ours, installed a landline, and told them to call us immediately if anything ever went wrong.

"We'll never call," my grandma dismissed. "We don't need help."

I left for college two months after that. During breaks, I visited home with suitcases full of toys, snacks, and games from the Chinatown in Flushing and the Union Square market. On rainy summer afternoons, I drove to them to Whole

Foods for vitamins and multigrain bread, and I entertained them with field trips to Ross and TJMaxx. After family dinners together, I brought out the mahjong set and coaxed them into playing a game or two before their bedtime. During these games, my grandparents played to win. They spoke rarely unless I asked them to tell me about the old times. I was happy to hear their stories; I was also worried that the people so willing to bet on my future once were now stuck living in the past.

This year, my grandparents turned eighty-one and eighty-three.

After another fall in the kitchen, my grandma can now barely sit upright for ten minutes without back pain. But when she can, she walks as if she were patrolling the school hallways and classrooms of Beijing again. She is a fussy, fragile, and irritable old woman, but still she carries her ninety-pound self with the grace and authority of a monarch. What she has lost in health and patience she makes up for tenfold in sass and charm. She wears black turtleneck sweaters and rhinestoned flats, even in the summer, and she hands out crisp hundred-dollar bills to my sister and me on every holiday to "get rid of pocket change." She goes to outlet stores not to save on clothes but to buy elephant statues and ceramic peacocks for her living room. And to prove she is still as alert and informed as ever, she spends at least ten minutes of each visit reciting either a play-by-play of the last NBA Rockets' game or the most recent anti-Communist agenda from WeChat, "just to keep the old brain working for a little while longer."

My grandpa, on the other hand, cares nothing for glamorous outfits and ceramic sculptures. He instead spends his time enjoying life by pretending none of his health problems exist. Despite his diabetes, he still eats more almond cookies and red bean mochis than my whole family combined when we visit buffets. Though he is almost entirely deaf, his room is littered with a collection of twenty some-odd speakers by Bose, Sony, UE Boom, and Beats to help him listen to music until he no longer can. He always asks for two things on his birthday—a new speaker and a large cake—and each year, he tells us they are better than the last.

My grandparents and I stopped playing mahjong two years ago. The last time I visited their house, I noticed the mahjong table was gone. The tiles were stowed away in the closet, their cracked leather pouch dusty from disuse.

"Lao Lao, do you not want to play anymore?" I asked.

"Oh, no no no. Look at how grown up you are! You're too busy for old people like us."

"But I'm free now!"

"No, no, I don't believe you," she said, ushering me to the door. "Don't you have work to do; didn't your mom need help with something; aren't you on your way to pick up food? Don't worry about us, we're fine here with our WeChat and our iPads."

"Do you want to play when I'm back?"

"No. We eat too slowly. And we won't want to sit after that. Your grandpa will need his nap. And my back will hurt."

Whenever my mom asks if they are okay, if they feel okay, my grandma scowls and brandishes her irreverence like an antidote against senility.

"I'm going to die any day now," she says at least once per visit. "My old bones can't handle much more anyway." When my mom protests, she cuts her off. "If you even think about sending me to hospice care, I'll kill myself before the doctors do. And then I'll kill you."

My grandpa agrees, but he says it with sentimentality. "Grandma is right," he echoes. "We would rather enjoy our time left at home and end on a happy note."

"Happy note with you, my wet ass," my grandma always cuts in before turning back to me. "But you get the gist. I'd rather die with my cats calling for me in my backyard and my ceramic pots by my bed than in the hospital. I bet you would, too."

Each time I listen to this conversation, I wonder when I will bring up my one last request: that some time when the three of us are all free, I want to play mahjong again. Before I ask, I will have the table set back up, the tiles already out, and a box of Magnum fudge bars waiting for my grandpa and me in the fridge. I will prop up the Houston Rockets cushion for my grandma's back and set out Velcro heating pads for my grandpa's knees. I will find an afternoon that I have completely free, and we will play like we once did when all three of us were young.

For our last game of mahjong together, I hope my grandma wins. I also hope that, when she wins, she does so with the same set of tiles that I laid out so many years ago on that rainy Saturday afternoon: *yi tiao long*—one long dragon. I hope she shows us her tiles and boasts that she has completed one long dragon—one long, full, rich life. I hope she collects her doubled winnings and feels like herself again—a monarch, a breadwinner, and the head of the household until the very end.

And then one inconsequential night after that, before she goes to bed, she will yell at my grandpa to turn off his godforsaken Communist music and tell him he's the don-key-shitting reason she's headed for the grave tomorrow, and she will turn off the lights for the last time and pass away peacefully in her sleep. On her way to heaven, a symphony of strings and brass instruments will play her the song they play for all deceased monarchs, and upon her arrival, she will get to play mahjong—or any game she wants—with me and my grandpa back like we did in the good old days. My grandpa will ask her to sit with him, and together, they will count their winnings as joint heads of the table, where they always have been and will be.

MR. BODDINGTON'S FIVE-YEAR MEMORY BOOK

———

In her famous essay "On Keeping a Notebook," Joan Didion confesses she keeps a private notebook not to keep an accurate factual record of her life, but to tell "what some would call lies." The lies are entries that fail to distinguish between what really happened and what *might* have happened, between how things are and how things *feel*.

In other words, Didion's notes are sporadic memories, oftentimes false, that are recorded only when she feels there is something worth remembering. In one note, she recalls having cracked crab for lunch the day her father came home from Detroit in 1945. In another, she revisits a conversation she overhears between a divorced woman and a bartender at a Wilmington hotel. When she rereads these entries years later, she is certain that both memories must be "embroidery" and make-believe. She writes that she could not have remembered the detail of cracked crab at ten years old, nor could she have known a woman's inner monologue in a bar.

Yet the fact these memories are wholly fabricated does not matter to Didion. Nor does it matter that the relevance of some notes—for instance, that "smart women almost always wear black in Cuba," or that "FACT: during 1964, 720 tons of soot fell on every square mile of New York City"—seem only marginal at best. What matters is simply that she wrote these notes down and, in doing so, wove them into the fabric of her life. Even if the notes are lies, they are important ones: lies that she deems meaningful for one reason or another, lies that—if stumbled across again years later, unexpectedly or accidentally—will make her feel a certain way, like the way an imaginary cracked crab reminds her of the afternoon her father came home bearing gifts, and she wept at the sight of him, and the two of them shared a bittersweet embrace of love and guilt.[16]

Like Didion, I also keep notebooks full of lies. I wrote my first entry when I was five years old. One day after school, I walked up to my mom, grabbed onto her shirt, and asked her why no one in my first grade class ever wanted to play with me at recess.

"Is it because no one likes me?"

"I like you!"

"You don't count."

Later that night, alone in my room, I tore out a sheet of paper from my spelling journal and asked again in purple colored pencil, "Why does no one like me?"

Perhaps this journal entry, like Didion's meal of cracked crab, is entirely fictitious. But when I recall that statement, that line—"Why does no one like me?"—I swear I can picture

---

16   Joan Didion, "On Keeping a Notebook," in *Slouching Towards Bethlehem* (New York: Farrar, Straus and Giroux, 1968), 131-141.

my mom's arms around me in the study room, my face buried in her lily-patterned Alfred Dunner shirt, my snot turning the pastel colors on her shoulder dark and gray. Even if this entry is a lie, the feelings of fear, loneliness, and childhood distress are not.

I like to believe my lack of friends at the age of five years old catalyzed my obsessive exploration of the question "why" and the subject matter "me." My heartache on the playground had been visceral and real; so had been my compulsive desire to write it away. Never mind that my exploration of personal feelings grew messier the longer I stayed in the maze. Here I am, still writing and reflecting in this chrysalis of self-consciousness, telling myself that one day I will somehow be able to turn any lie into the truth.

I filled up my first notebook the summer after third grade. My friend Tory gave it to me in the carpool lane, along with the cordial suggestion that I keep in touch with her even after school let out. Of course, with a private journal on hand, I became more interested in the idea of keeping in touch with myself.

I wrote sporadically until middle school. I thought if I did not write about the sixth, seventh, and eighth grade, I could more easily forget about the chubby girl who wore navy polo shirts and red pleated skirts to school each day, who made the B team in every sport and made up for physical weakness with academic arrogance. There was no place in my journal for the twelve-year-old girl who cried upon receiving a 96 on an earth science test because it "was not high enough." Of course, the fact that I can still picture this hysterical girl crying in the backseat of the car, my mom laughing at her all the while, tells me how much she still haunts me.

In high school, I promised myself I would regularly write about the person I was becoming, whether she was attractive company or not. Since then, I have filled up ten more notebooks documenting my coming of age. Most of them are 160-page, college-lined journals by Peter Pauper Press. All of them, save the one I am using now, are stacked neatly in my closet, where they will likely collect dust until the day I move out and stumble upon the past again. Each notebook was an inconclusive attempt to understand myself at the time of writing. Now, each notebook is an intimate recollection of the person I used to be.

I imagine note keeping gives off the appearance that I am self-absorbed. If so, it is because I am. All writers reckon with this truth at one point or another: in observing the world, we can examine it only by first studying our own. Keepers of notebooks in particular approach our craft with a certain vanity, a certain belief that our own naked "I" matters enough to be explored again and again. Of all writers, we are the most egocentric. We believe that writing privately about the world will somehow make it better. We store notebooks in hidden, secretive places at home; allegedly, we are protecting them until the day they serve some latent purpose.

I keep a notebook because the physical act of writing in private gives me a sense of accomplishment. Taking on a task no one has asked me to makes me feel like a more diligent, dutiful person. As with a Samaritan who does good anonymously, it is the self-induced sense of righteousness that matters to me. I also keep a notebook to provide a sense of comfort. If the future is unknown, I would like to at least be able to hold onto the memorabilia of the past. My notes are gateways to former identities, tangible proof that old versions of myself once existed. And if old ones can exist, new ones can surely appear.

For all these reasons, I keep a notebook. The entries are useful only accidentally, sporadically, and only to me, so I tell myself I *must* be self-absorbed in order to keep going. I tell myself there is some meaning to recording my individual truth, even if that means telling myself lies.

On January 22, 2017, I started my thirteenth notebook. It is small enough to fit in my palm, and its thick cover is dotted with pastel prints of bicycles, eyeglasses, keys, thumbtacks, and horseshoes. The notebook has its own name: Mr. Boddington's Five-Year Memory Book. It is lined with 365 pages, featuring five years per page and five lines per day. The format of the book is such that, if I were to flip to the page entitled "January 22," I would see five years of entries from that day spanning the years 2017 through 2021.

This memory book was given to me by a college friend I no longer talk to but whom I think about every time I write in it. My first entry begins with his words: "I am excited to see what you write in five years." At the time, I felt excited, too. Though I would be keeping two notebooks simultaneously— one for daily diary entries and one for the kind of sporadic note keeping that Didion loves—I was eager to experiment with something new.

That day, I began writing my longest lie yet. It is one continuous lie of omission: rather than recording the make-believe, I promised myself that Mr. Boddington would only see the things that made me happy each day.

I imagine many people—writers, especially—find this kind of note keeping wildly disingenuous. If writing is, as Kafka says, the "axe for the frozen sea within us," then keeping a gratitude journal is the naïve attempt to hold that sea together.[17] I, too, often question the intentions I have for keeping Mr. Boddington around. It is one thing to record the day's events even if they are not interesting; it is another thing altogether to record only the good ones to paint one's days—which, of course, make up one's life—into perfection. My attempt to be grateful each day is an exercise in impossibility. No journal can make me forget that somber moments exist.

Mr. Boddington does, however, help me forget most of them.

Some entries across the years include:

"Took a nap at my grandparents' house after playing mahjong with them" (March 27, 2018);
"Woke up at 7:50 a.m. for Clinton Street pancakes with Francis" (July 6th, 2019); and
"Opened the windows at night, fell asleep to rustling leaves and fragrance" (April 12, 2020).

In accordance with the self-imposed rules of my book, I do exactly what Didion warns against: record the day's events

---

17   Franz Kafka, *Letters to Friends, Family and Editors*, trans. by Richard and Clara Winston, (New York: Schocken Books, 1977), 16.

exactly as I experience them. But with such limited space, I memorialize only the most beautiful facts at the time. It is no longer possible for me to remember anything that happened on March 27, 2018 other than my nap at my grandparents' place and that there had been "really calming before-the-storm grey skies and a cool breeze." The same goes for July 6, 2019, and April 12, 2020, for which the only other notes I have written are that I "watched my friends perform at the Javitz Center for KCON" and "took a night walk with my mother in fifty-degree weather," respectively.

In leaving out certain memories in favor of others, I am choosing to consciously forget. I am also acknowledging that, while most of my past will fade to dust, there are certain fragments I am willing to relive again and again. While I agree with Didion—a laundry list of the day's events would indeed be rather pointless and boring to the extreme—Mr. Boddington's book is no ordinary list. It is a series of deliberate omissions, a narration of compassionate lies that tells me if joy and the recognition of it are my past, they are also what my future holds. In comparing my twelfth and thirteenth notebooks side by side, I must confess that selective truth is more interesting than the make-believe.

But Mr. Boddington leaves me with one other conundrum. I started my thirteenth notebook while still writing in my twelfth from time to time, and the truth is, it is difficult to keep up with two notebooks simultaneously. After my five years with Mr. Boddington, perhaps I should bid his kind goodbye. Perhaps it is redundant to keep two journals, one in which I tell the fictitious truth, and the other in which I tell honest lies. I might merge the notebooks into one, where the entries matter only to the extent that I feel something when writing (and possibly rereading) them. Or I might forget about journaling altogether and just live life as it presents itself to me—a raw and unedited reality.

But then again, journaling is not so much about falsifying reality as it is about interpreting it in an instinctive, implacable, and personal way. I cherish Mr. Boddington so because the more entries I write, the more indispensable my past entries become. On May 17, 2019, I visited my high school to catch up with my teachers. When I later wrote that "we talked for four hours," I realized I had visited them on the same day last year—a reminder of their ongoing presence in my life. On April 29, 2020, I talked with my best friend Caitlyn on the phone about my upcoming Fulbright grant in Taiwan. On the same day last year, we had shared Impossible Burgers at The Quantum Leap to talk about what life after college might look like. Moments like these are where I feel most comforted by my writing. Coincidences or not, I see these occasions as evidence that there is, indeed, some narrative thread weaving its way through an otherwise arbitrary life.

There are also days where past events I have recorded end up influencing how I feel in the present. On December 9, 2019, I walked into the coffee shop Whistle & Fizz, ordered a black sesame latte, and sat at the counter with Mr. Boddington's Book in hand. I had just flown back to New York after my semester abroad in Singapore, and I was picking up refreshments before visiting friends at NYU. As I waited for my name to be called, I flipped open the book and began skimming through the past. Suddenly, a familiar voice called out.

"Amy?" I looked up to see a boy in a V-neck and black baseball cap holding my drink in his hand. It was Wes—the friend who had given me Mr. Boddington three years ago.

"Wes!" I leaned over the counter to give him a hug. When I sat back down, I lifted the book in my hand. "Remember this?"

"You're still using it?"

"Of course."

We talked for two more hours after that. He asked a friend to cover his shift and sat next to me by the counter, serving me free samples of cold brew lemonade, green apple fizz, and nitro mango tea as we caught up like old friends. What exactly we talked about, I no longer remember—perhaps the never-ending search for new jobs and good friends, or how busy we had been.

Time changes everything. Our conversation was pleasant, mature, and had all the sincerity and seriousness of soon-to-be college graduates, but it was nothing like the conversations we shared years ago. As we looked toward our futures, I found myself reminiscing about our past. I thought back to the one evening in Salzburg where, after slipping on cobblestones and getting drenched in the rain, we had shared dinner together while listening to a Mozart symphony at The Baroque Hall St. Peter (September 2, 2017). I saw us as eighteen-year-olds again, running around Washington Square Park on an NYU-declared snow day, laughing as we fought our first snowball fight in the city a hundred steps from where we sat now in the coffee shop (February 9th, 2017).

As I said goodbye to Wes, I said goodbye to our younger selves and our saccharine past. I thanked him for the drink and the book, and I left Whistle & Fizz feeling wistful but glad. After all these years, Mr. Boddington had indeed kept his promise to me: I felt grateful remembering only our good times together, one of which was simply that we had crossed paths.

In placing my memories with both Mr. Boddington and Peter Pauper over the years, I have addressed my feelings of preemptive nostalgia and allayed my fears of forgetting the past. I have assigned individual meaning to scattered memories, random factoids, long conversations, and even sentimental lies. If the intention of keeping a notebook is truly, as Didion says, to keep on nodding terms with the people I used to be, then my notes have, at the very least, kept my past selves alive.

Whether I will continue to keep two notebooks at once, I am not sure. I simply hope to keep writing. Publicly, privately, something, anything. I will construct meaning in my attempt to write it down, and through my beautiful lies—both by creation and by omission—I will pin down the significance of an otherwise insignificant life.

TWENTY-ONE
YEARS YOUNG

———

"There will always be children and there will always be old people. We spend most of our lives somewhere in between ... but of course each of us is infinite."
—ELIZABETH ALEXANDER, *THE LIGHT OF THE WORLD*[18]

One.

There are two pieces of advice I will remember from the summer of 2017. One was given to me by a 32-year-old coworker, a South African woman whose dresses were the colors of canaries and whose earrings were the size of her smile. She was a grant writer at The Andrew W. Mellon Foundation; I was an investment analyst. I told her that, after working in finance twice and despising it, I did not know what I was doing with my life, nor what I would do next.

"I get it," she had replied. "I worked at an investment bank for ten years before coming here. The fact that you want to leave after two summers—good for you! And in any case,

———

18 Elizabeth Alexander, T*he Light of the World: A Memoir* (New York: Grand Central Publishing, 2016), 156-160.

careers aren't made of years, Amy. They're made of decades. Two summers is nothing. Especially if you're working for, what, the next forty or fifty years?"

I nodded, mostly to convince myself I understood.

"The point is, if there's ever a time to make crazy choices and crazy mistakes, it's now. If you want to leave, leave! If you want to stay, great. No one's stopping you. No choice is the wrong choice unless you're choosing nothing at all. Socrates said that. Just kidding! But let's pretend he did."

Two.

It is August 9 and I am flying home to see family. I am congratulating myself on a summer well-spent in New York—I did not get fired from my job, I watched Seth Meyers bake strawberry vanilla cake with Martha Stewart live, I got better at telling my eating disorder (instead of my dietitian) to fuck off—and now I am thinking about all the things I can do back home and all the things I will do again when I return to the city.

As the plane takes off, I lean down to grab my book when I spot a woman across the aisle flipping through a stack of papers. Pleasantly surprised to have found a fellow reading buddy, I stick my head out further only to make out the words: "CREMATION SCHEDULING POLICY."

Oh.

I look away, feeling sorry for her loss and sorry for my intrusion. I lean as far back in my economy seat as I can, which is not that far at all before the kid behind me starts pummeling the back with his feet. I flip to page 194 of David Sedaris' *Calypso.* I close my eyes, thinking.

I am thinking how strange it is that this woman and I are both on a flight home presumably to visit family, except everyone I want to see is still alive. I am thinking how strange it must feel to fly somewhere not to greet the living but to part with the dead. I am thinking how not everything in life is a choice.

Three.

The second piece of advice I will remember from the summer was given to me by Elizabeth Alexander, the president of The Andrew W. Mellon Foundation, an educator of thirty years, a mother of two sons, and a self-prescribed "tough love" kind of lover.

We are having tea in her office one afternoon, and I ask her about her career in writing.

"How did you become a writer? How did you just decide one day that that's what you wanted to be?"

She sets down her teacup and looks at me with an expression that tells me my questions should be self-explanatory.

"There is no secret formula, Amy. Everything boils down to hard work and one simple belief: If you must, you will."

Four.

I am thinking that I have been alive for two decades now. That is a little over 10,512,000 minutes. A bit longer than 630,720,000 seconds.

If the average life expectancy for a female born in the United States is approaching eighty years, then—assuming I am the average—I have about 31,536,000 "just a minute"s left to ask for. 1,892,160,000 "just a second"s to reflect on the rest of my life.

Assuming sleep and daily routines account for the majority of those seconds, I figure I do not have much time left at all. It is terrifying and humbling to recognize there is a limit to the days I have to pause and think and figure out just exactly who I am and how are you and what I want and where we are and where we are all going and why.

Five.

As I head toward baggage claim, I am thinking about "The Neptune Society," which was the only other thing I could make out from her cremation papers before looking away. When I get home, I look up the name and find it is the largest provider of affordable cremation services in the nation, with over forty years of experience in carrying out people's final wishes with dignity and respect.

How funny it is that some people claim to be seasoned professionals at handling death when no one understands it.

Six.

I attended my first funeral six years ago.

I remember three things from the service: my childhood friend and her father crying as they gave her mother's eulogy; the procession toward the coffin and how we rose from our pews, streaming down the center aisle like grains of sand trickling through the opening of an hourglass; and the burial chest, where on top of a bed of white sheets and bouquets of lilies, daisies, and orchids, lay someone who had recently died.

It is strange to see a dead person after spending so many years with them alive. It is strange to see skin the color of white marble and lips a bruised shade of blue. It is strange to see death in the flesh before even registering death as an idea, to see someone with her hands by her side, her eyes closed, her hair combed and parted perfectly lying in a coffin, and wonder how someone can make death look beautiful.

Funerals are a strange affair. They celebrate life in the aftermath of death. They replace tangible presence with intangible memories. They honor a person's stories by putting them on public display, all at once, as if the more slideshows and collages and eulogies there are, the more a dead person can remain alive. Perhaps strangest of all is that funerals are a formal acknowledgment of grief, a professional cavalcade of mourning expressed through a sea of black dresses and suits, expensive program leaflets, candles and acolytes and flowers and organ music resonating from within a church.

There must be some therapeutic value in rethinking one's own life in the aftermath of another's. There must also be some therapeutic value in doing so as a group.

I once heard that funerals are held for the living. I believe it.

Seven.

At what age do people stop celebrating birthdays and start fearing them? Tomorrow is my mom's birthday, and though I cannot wait to celebrate her with presents and cake, she will certainly remind us that August 10 is no longer a noteworthy day.

"I hate today," my mother will proclaim. She will eat her cake and ask for seconds and also say, "I am too old to be eating this." She will look at my sister and me and ask, suddenly and urgently, "When will I get to buy cake for my grandchildren?"

My mom did not always talk like this on her birthday.

Perhaps my mom hates birthdays because somewhere between youth and old age, there exists a stretch of time in our lives where things plateau, where life stops feeling exciting. Our days become a routine. Our birthdays become an unwelcome reminder that indifference is suffocating.

I fear the day my birthday stops being exciting. I fear becoming an adult who, when asked how things are going, says, "Not much. Just work."

I want work to be more than "just" work. I want life to be more than "not much." If, one day, I wake up convinced this is too much to ask for, then there is no better time to ask for more than now, on the youngest day of the rest of my life.

Eight.

My friends approaching their thirties sometimes confess to me that college was the last time life felt interesting. Post-college life, they tell me, is like one steady jog on a treadmill. After a course is selected at random, the machine begins whirring at a steady incline, and the pace is just fast enough that no one ever steps off, for fear of getting left behind.

I fear getting on the treadmill more than I fear getting left behind.

I fear if I get on, I will trudge along to a few popular programs for years without ever asking why. I fear I will grow up and grow old walking on that treadmill until I turn thirty, forty, fifty, and I am married, and I have a house in the suburbs and two kids in private school and a stable job where work is just okay—where everything in life is just okay—and I go to sleep one night wondering where, exactly, along the treadmill did things stop moving me—was it when I got on or when I decided I would never get off—and when did the years in between become ensnared and lost in L'Engle's wrinkle in time?

Perhaps this is what adults mean when they talk about undergoing a midlife crisis.

Nine.

I do not want to live life in a state of euphoria; I only want to live as if the idea of euphoria exists.

Some things that feel euphoric: hugging my parents when they pick me up at the airport; sunrise from Jinmian Mountain in Taipei; smelling my grandfather's childhood blanket; half-price Wednesdays at Dave & Buster's; sending and receiving handwritten letters; volcano cakes from Rainforest Cafe; October in New York City and Cinque Terre; and dancing on stage or in the rain.

Euphoria also exists as some far-off cloud nine, an amorphous anticipation for things I have not yet done but hope to someday. Things like giving the toast at my sister's wedding, holding my first child, or traveling to all seven continents only to realize I am most content at home.

As I tumble into adulthood, I hope to never lose sight of the things that make me excited to be alive. The chance to encounter paradise on earth, even accidentally, makes life worth living until the end. Perhaps, if I avoid the treadmill in favor of serendipity and chance, I will not fear the day my own ashes are scattered by The Neptune Society.

Ten.

I am walking in Bellaire Park with my older sister, and we are catching each other up about our summers when I ask her how medical school has been. She tells me it has been exhausting as usual. She says this with a smile on her face. She then goes on to explain something new she has learned in her interactive patient sessions.

"You know how some people in their forties and fifties go to therapy or seek psychiatric help because they're freaking out about some midlife crisis?" She says this with "midlife crisis" in air quotes.

I nod. I think about it all the time.

"Well, we were told in lecture the other day to stop calling it a 'midlife crisis.' Now, Baylor is teaching all of its med students to call it a 'midlife transition.' It makes sense. I'm actually surprised we didn't make the switch sooner. I don't know why it's a 'crisis' to rethink how we want to spend the rest of our lives. It seems like a normal thing to do, to take a step back and reflect."

"Right, so instead of saying I'm having an identity crisis, I could just say I'm transitioning to a new set of values to live by. Ooh, or that I'm transforming. Like a butterfly. Sounds nice."

"Right."

Eleven.

I hate the "life is a treadmill" analogy. I hate to think that I could be looking forward my entire life and still end up nowhere.

Twelve.

If life were a treadmill—a steady progression of predictable and linear events—I would not have attended my first funeral before my first wedding.

But because I know the former, I feel like I already know what to expect in the latter: the formal dresses and suits, the sea of warm candles and white flowers, the symbols of faith and purity and the church, the resonating music, the teary-eyed speeches, the families seated in rows and brought together in celebration of life.

Strange how that works—how looking backwards is what keeps me moving forward.

Thirteen.

When I turned thirteen, I remember wanting to stay thirteen forever, because up until that point everyone kept telling me that turning thirteen was the biggest deal in the world, and I liked feeling like I was a big deal, which wasn't hard as an eighth grader roaming the halls of St. John's Middle School but seemed quite impossible at the Upper School across the street.

When I turned sixteen, I remember wanting to stay sixteen forever, because that year for my "sweet 16" I went to Dave & Buster's with my entire family and ordered pretzel dogs and cheeseburger sliders and hot sugared donut holes for lunch and played every arcade game at least twice and won myself a blender after three years of accumulated tickets, and I wondered when was the last time I could shamelessly play at an arcade like this with everyone I loved and not feel self-conscious.

When I turned twenty-one, I remember wanting to stay twenty-one forever, because it was only my third week of my exchange semester at the National University of Singapore, and somehow I found myself in the third floor lounge of University Town's South Tower sharing yuzu and lime and salted caramel and eight other flavors of cheesecake from Cat & the Fiddle with seven new friends, and as we played Overcooked and Super Smash Bros on someone's Nintendo Switch, I remember feeling like this was it, the best birthday I could ever wish for—having just landed on the other side of the world and already feeling on top of it.

Fourteen.

The age I still thought my world was *the* world, and everyone was looking at it, appraising it, passing judgments and expectations as if no one had anything else better to do, as if no one looked at their own worlds the same way and only gave a shit about mine to the extent that it might affect their own.

Fifteen.

The age I watched my sister leave for college and realized there was a whole ocean to lose myself in outside of our little fishbowl.

Sixteen.

The age I lost myself in an eating disorder worrying too much about what other people thought of my world, which ended up being both the most painful and the most necessary misstep in my attempt to find answers about meaning, purpose, and how to live a good life.

Seventeen.

The number of books I read the year I began anorexia rehabilitation. Each of these books touched on the value of time and of aging. *Kitchen Confidential* by Anthony Bourdain, for instance, taught me that aging is an art, that good things take time to form, but when crafted with patience, cream rises. *The Catcher in the Rye* by J. D. Salinger urged me to start forming that cream now because one day when I am older, I will suddenly start missing everybody—terribly and all at once. *Infinite Jest* by David Foster Wallace reassured me I do not have to be old to know life is sometimes an ugly, painful affair, but that regardless of age, compassion is always an over-the-counter antidote. And *Their Eyes Were Watching God* by Zora Neale Hurston convinced me that no matter how dark the horizon looms ahead, the sun carries with it new light each day that can rebuild the world.

In other words, aging is anything we want it to be. It is an inevitable loss; it is also a privilege and a gift. It is a reminder that all things come to an end; it is also a harbinger of suffering, love, regret, loss, grief, nostalgia, joy, and every other feeling that makes us human.

What remains consistent across the books I read is this: aging is an unparalleled curator of perspective.

Calypso by David Sedaris speaks directly to this point. In his essay "The Comey Memo," Sedaris stumbles across a half dozen photos of his family taken on Emerald Isle in 1981, and with his brothers, sisters, and him ranging in age from twelve to twenty-four, he notes that everything about those photos "is golden, literally," from their tans to their outlooks on the future.[19] He points out that things are different in middle age. It is not that we turn pessimistic, per se; we simply have a sharpened sense of urgency, a narrower outlook, a stronger hunch that our "golden days" are finite.

Not that I want to rush this shift in perspective, because, according to Sedaris, the "golden days" is a period I have only just begun.

Eighteen.
The problem with enjoying "golden days" is that it is difficult to enjoy them in a vacuum. As a kid, I found that gold diminished in value the instant I started comparing how

---

19   David Sedaris, "The Comey Memo," in *Calypso* (New York: Little, Brown and Company, 2018), 252.

golden my days were to everyone else's. I spent most of middle school through college surrounded by the competitive chaos that fuels Chinatown, and oftentimes, when I was not careful, I found myself chasing after fool's gold in the form of Instagrammed beauty and Forbes 30 Under 30 labels and Ivy League college degrees and everything else that I suspect will fade to nothing when I die but, at the time, were things I was dying to have.

Nineteen.

The age when all my neurotic tendencies and media-induced insecurities caught up to me. The age I was recommended Lexapro and Prozac and Celexa and other SSRIs to "fix" the parts of me falling into anxiety and depression and general "mental instability." The age when a physician and two dietitians and two therapists pointed out that my attempts to recreate someone else's halcyon days led instead to the deterioration of my own.

At nineteen, I was taught by medical professionals how to coax myself out of mental hellholes while accepting that they exist. Once I accepted this, I discovered that most everyone around me was struggling with their own hellholes, too, and I felt simultaneously heartbroken and relieved to know I was not alone in my spells of madness. So, in a way, the darkest seconds of my life paved the way for some of the best. If anxiety-induced anorexia is the reason I spent four years of my life feeling aged and fatigued, my journey toward recovery is the reason why I now feel lucky to feel young again.

Twenty.

In addition to being my former boss at The Andrew W. Mellon Foundation, Elizabeth Alexander—the woman who gave me the advice "if you must, you will"—is an educator, a scholar, and a memoirist. She is also a distinguished poet who, in 2009, wrote and delivered Barack Obama's inauguration poem "Praise Song for the Day."

I remember reading the poem the day she joined the foundation. I read it again the morning before having tea with her, and since then, I have reread it many more times. My favorite lines are still the same—the entirety of the last two stanzas—in which she proclaims that anything can be crafted or promised or brought forth again, if only we have the courage to begin.

When I think about this message in last two stanzas, I think about her friendship with Barack and Michelle Obama, about her dedication to the humanities, about her lectures in poetry and African American studies for the past twenty years—all of which has convinced her that belief in education, in curiosity, and in people, is everything. I think about our conversation in her office, during which she told me in the most unapologetic way possible that the only way to walk forward into the dark was to believe I could. I think about how she believed in her own lines at President Obama's inauguration, and how her confidence inspired others to believe, too.

Twenty-One.

If there is one thing I believe in now, it is that I have needed every second I have lived so far to become the person I am. Twenty-one years old. Twenty-one years young. "Only" about 1,892,160,000 seconds left to write about it.

But if life is one continuous story, I am in no rush to spell out the end. As with any plot, there are overarching moments that capture its essence. I am still in search of these junctures, these occasions that bring me closest to and furthest from temporary ecstasy on cloud nine. Perhaps I am too young to weave this patchwork of stories together, but at twenty-one years young, at least I am not afraid to try.

This patchwork of essays is only the beginning, the first draft of many. It is also the best draft I have. Everything I write here is full of holes and question marks, which is my honest truth so far. As I grow up and grow old, my understanding of reality will surely change. As it does, I hope to write and rewrite this story many times over, so much so that by the time my own end is near, and the bouquets are being ordered, and the church is being reserved, and the people I love are flying home with cremation scheduling policies in their own hands preparing eulogies to say goodbye, they will know what to say.

WHEN WE STOP BEING IMMORTAL

———

One month into my eating disorder recovery, I picked up Atul Gawande's book, *Being Mortal: Medicine and What Matters Most in the End,* from my shelf. I let out a chuckle. How ironic it was to read a book titled *Being Mortal* the week after my physician had told me I was lucky to be alive. Elaine, my older sister, was the one who gave it to me. It was—like many meaningful things in life—an accident. She did not like the book at all; she barely read half of it before placing it on my bookshelf.

"I liked the general premise, but the stories were a little too sappy for me."

"Well, good thing I love that stuff." I tried to laugh at myself in a performance of self-pity. I lay in bed and imagined what the next few months would look like between battling my anorexia and dealing with my terrified parents. Elaine came over and sat on my covers.

"Amy, everything is going to be okay."

"Yeah, I know," I mumbled, shrugging away from her and looking at the ceiling. "I just want to be alone."

"Okay." She stood up and paused before leaving the room.

"It's okay, by the way. To be sad. And to be sappy. Sentimentality isn't a bad thing. You just care a little bit too much sometimes. Anyway, I hope the book helps you process what you're going through right now. It might help you fight the little person in your brain."

"How?"

She shrugged. "Just a feeling."

When I first opened *Being Mortal*, I expected the average diatribe against elderly care in America—a book that shook its head at the failures of the US healthcare system, a book that harped on the obvious. I expected pages drowned in dull research the way pancakes are drowned (and then ruined) in molasses. I expected an author who thought that, in writing with the syrupy language of medical jargon, something would eventually stick.

I started the book with skepticism. I skimmed the introduction and turned up my nose. I hoped for literary mediocrity and generalized one-liners I could laugh at—the kind one might find in medical journals whose insubstantial editorial tag lines range anywhere from "We define and redefine professionalism" (*The Journal of the American Medical Association*) to "If you don't like it, we'll retract it!" (*The Lancet*).[20]

But somewhere between the first and fourth chapter, I stopped pretending to be bored. My grip on the pages and on his stories tightened. My hand reached for my pen, and I began inserting my own life in the blanks between

---

20 Michel Accad, MD, "A Guide to Top Medical Journals: A Primer for Healthcare Journalists," *Alert and Oriented* (blog), April 6, 2016.

paragraphs. By the sixth chapter, *Being Mortal* had sparked in me the first of many conscious attempts to find out, once and for all, what mattered in life. Gawande convinced me that life itself mattered—which would have seemed a little silly and melodramatic and cliché, of course, had I not recently come so close to losing it.

Gawande spent most of the book exploring nursing homes and their failure to improve the conditions of patients they claimed to treat. Nursing homes, he observed, devoted themselves above all to safety, which meant prioritizing strict, sterilized routines over the kind of livelihood that offered purpose and sparked autonomous joy. Through hard conversations with his own patients and family, Gawande found that, in the end, what they wanted most was not security but freedom and responsibility—the ability to make their own meals, choose their own hobbies, take care of their own pets, and so on, regardless of whether these were considered "dangerous" to their health or not. What really mattered in the end, then, was the opportunity not to live a good death, but a good life.

But what was a good life? As someone who recently felt robbed of one, I needed to know. I thought I might find the answers in Gawande's interactions with his elderly patients. Instead, I found them in a conversation he details between himself and a young woman named Laura Carstensen. At the age of twenty-one, Carstensen suffered a car accident that left her barely alive. With a serious head injury, internal bleeding, and multiple shattered bones, she spent several months in the hospital coming in and out of consciousness. When she finally got well enough to make sense of her surroundings, she realized that besides herself, the only other patients in her ward were elderly women whose legs were strung in the air due to hip fractures. The whole scene felt, in her words, "cartoonish."[21]

That was how reality felt for me, too. Everything felt strange when a physician diagnosed me with anorexia and told me I should have experienced cardiac arrest long ago. She told me I should have felt relieved, but instead, I was angry, bitter, and in deep despair. With college put on pause, I was forced to face the reality that daily life, which was once full of endless possibilities, would now be spent fighting to stay alive. I suddenly found myself surrounded by doctors and therapists instead of professors and classmates. I found myself playing with rubber broccoli on plastic plates instead of eating with friends. I found myself curled up in bed during life's supposed prime, crying over Gawande's reminder that I was not, in fact, immortal.

But my proximity to death also made me keenly aware that, despite my bitterness and fear of the future, I was lucky to be alive. Once I had accepted this fact, I began obsessing over the most mundane rituals of daily life. That spring, with little to do and too much time to think, my priorities shifted to the minutiae of the here and now, to the pleasure in small, everyday things: The texture of my tattered childhood blanket as I stared at old family photos. The smell of St. Augustine grass after it rained. The warmth of the sun flooding through living room windows, and the brilliant kaleidoscopes of light it made when its white rays passed through oak leaves. I

---

21   Atul Gawande, *Being Mortal: Medicine and What Matters in the End* (New York: Picador, 2014), 96.

began looking forward to breakfast in the morning and slow walks down South Rice Boulevard with my parents at night. I enjoyed the hours I spent talking to my sister, mostly about nothing. And for the first time, I enjoyed the days I spent *doing* nothing. As someone who approached life as an exercise of neuroticism, I had forgotten how wonderful it was to take a break from the mania.

At a time when I wanted to believe in nothing but a limitless future, I reached some kind of end. I had gone to Europe to see my horizons expand past infinity. I came back and witnessed their collapse. But as I sat home alone, cradling Gawande's book to my chest, I felt calm and strangely content. The future had indeed contracted ahead of me, finite and uncertain. But these limits provided a sense of urgency from which burst an intense, euphoric clarity. Because I had felt life at its most fragile, I wanted every day afterwards to matter. I decided then that I wanted a life of meaning—one in which each day revolved around a cause worth sacrificing for and people worth living for.

In the latter half of spring, I stopped thinking about missed classes and only called my closest friends. I turned off social media; then I turned off my phone. I sent an occasional letter or two (selfishly, to process my own thoughts), but mostly, I spent my days surrounded by family and books, doing only the things that mattered to me.

By summertime, I felt distinctly grateful for reality as I knew it. I did not mind that there were many things in my life I had not yet achieved. I was too busy holding on to what I had not lost. My near-death experience, like Carstensen's, made me realize what I cherished was not the entire world, but only the everyday pleasures and people around me.

For the first time in my life, I understood that at any moment, they could be gone.

Carstensen summed up my feelings in one simple hypothesis: "How we seek to spend our time depends on how much time we think we have left."[22]

That was it. The lightbulb above my head, the "aha" moment, the key to a good life. It was not age that mattered, but perspective. It was why the young prefer talking about the future rather than the past. For them, the good life revolves around the idea that "the world is your oyster," "the sky is the limit," and so on. But to people who think they have much less time to live, these grandiose statements are illusions and false hopes. Their good life instead lies in the past and present as opposed to a future that may not come. It was why Carstensen, after spending months coming to terms with her own fragility after the car crash, empathized with the elderly patients around her who professed needs only for "everyday comforts, for companionship."[23]

When I read that passage in Gawande's book, I starred and circled it so urgently in black ink that I tore through the page.

Carstensen's theory on perspective was, for me, *Being Mortal*'s opening act. All of Gawande's subsequent stories cascaded from it. When he spoke of ninety-year-old patients with failing respiratory systems and intestinal tumors, he was not just writing about the significance of age. He was writing about the significance of time, and how meaningful it was to recognize how much of it we have left.

---

22 Gawande, *Being Mortal*, 97.
23 Gawande, *Being Mortal*, 100.

When I was diagnosed with anorexia, I was confronted with the terrifying truth that my immortality was only an illusion. Gawande's book reassured me this was only the first lesson to learn. The second was this: *being mortal is good.*

As a young person, I believed in all those clichés about reaching for the stars. Things changed when an unfavorable medical diagnosis grounded me, forcing me to reckon with my own mortality earlier than most do. In five short months, my priorities shifted from putting my stamp on the world to narrowing in on the here and now. Now that I have finished college, however, things have slowly started to shift back. For better or worse, I am still fighting to retain that image of romantic, idealistic, even naïve, youth. Perspective, like life itself, seems to be one long balancing act.

Not that more optimism or hope is wrong. I am fortunate enough to still have both. This is what illnesses do: make you feel lucky in spite of all the suffering they cause. They make you painfully aware of everything you had before and everything you still have after, and though some things are lost and others will never be the same, what remains is golden.

The musings of an involuntary gap semester, for instance, will stay with me for life, as will the late-night talks I shared with Carstensen and Gawande. They are both pen pals to whom I address occasional existential concerns, when everything around me is still and everyone I love is asleep. Even now, on days when a feverishly expanding traffic jam of thoughts draws me away from reality, I scribble and scrawl to them in the margins of my imagination, asking all the impossible questions I dare to ask about being mortal.

I am mortal, I am young, and the fact I can now recognize both makes life even more precious. Limits, which I once saw as purely restrictive, are now paradoxically freeing.

Now, they run my imagination wild as I wade neck-deep in the tail end of youth.

I have one reoccurring dream in which I am fifty years older and a new grandmother. In this dream, I am always sitting in the living room of a warm home, playing a game like Go Fish or Connect Four with my grandchildren. My sister is playing with us, and my children are in the kitchen making braised pork ribs and ground pork pancakes—family recipes my parents taught them years ago. I must still be in Houston because a pair of mockingbirds is perched on an oak tree outside, caroling for us through an open window, and I can hear the distant purring of cars going down a highway I somehow know is I-69. I must still be in the same home too, for I am sitting in a wooden chair that is identical to the one I sat in as a nineteen-year-old.

At the end of the dream, I always sigh a deep, happy sigh. I always wake up when my kids tell me it is time to eat. Sometimes I wake up in tears. I promise myself I will eat all I can when that time comes.

Despite the uncertainties that lie ahead, I tell myself this future surely exists, and that I still have time left to make it my own. How much time, I will never know, but I tell myself I am lucky: lucky to be alive and lucky to still have dreams like this.

THE MAN WITH THE MAGICAL WATCH

———

My favorite bedtime story is one my mom told me when I was a teenager and thought I knew everything. In English, the story is called "The Man with the Magical Watch."

It goes like this.

———

The man with the magical watch was an ordinary man. He was kind, hardworking, and wished for a better tomorrow each day. Like everyone else, he was very curious to see how life would unfold around him. At times, he wished he could see the future.

His ordinary life was filled with the ordinary ups and downs of a twenty-five-year old. He went to work, he hung out with friends, he alternated between calling parents and going out on the weekends. For the most part, life was good. Now all he wanted was someone to share it with.

And then one day, the man met the love of his life. On one ordinary night of drinking and dancing with his friends, he saw her from across the room, laughing, twirling in a beautiful red gown that made every other dress fade away. He felt silly walking up to her, but when he asked her to dance, she said yes.

That one word made the man feel extraordinary for the rest of the evening. The two of them danced and talked for hours about everything and nothing. The night was almost perfect. The man only wished he could have met her sooner. He knew then that he really liked her. He felt she liked him, too. He said he hoped to see her again. She said, "I'd like that."

That evening, the ordinary man went home and made a wish.

"Please let me know if I will get to see her again," he prayed. "Please let me know if, one day, we will end up together, if that woman will become my wife."

He knew he sounded crazy, and that everything about that night had been crazy, but he closed his eyes anyway and repeated his wish over and over again until he fell asleep. Later that night, an angel appeared in his dreams. The angel spoke:

"Because you have been a kind, hardworking man in this life and have never asked for anything as much as you have asked for this, I will grant you your wish." The angel brought out a watch that looked as ordinary as he did.

"This watch is a magical watch," the angel went on. "If you turn the minute hand forward, you will be able to turn forward time. An hour forward on the watch is a year forward in life. You can skip forward to any point in your future and see where life has taken you. You will be able to see if you marry the girl you love, if you have a family, if you grow up and grow old together. But be mindful of one thing: this watch cannot be turned back. Any time you skip will be time foregone."

The man so desperately wanted to know if he would see the girl again that he told the angel, "I am willing to give up time for her." And so he accepted the deal and took the watch from the angel's hand.

When the man woke up, the magical watch was already on his wrist. To test if the angel had spoken the truth, he closed his eyes and moved the second hand forward ever so slightly. When he opened his eyes, the sky outside was no longer a soft pale blue but black as ink. His heart thumped against his chest.

He closed his eyes again and turned forward the hour hand the equivalent of seven years. He always knew he wanted to be married by the age of thirty-two. He needed to know who it was. The man woke up next to someone else. When he turned to see who it was, he began to cry. It was the girl of his dreams.

The man was so happy that he never thought once about the seven years he had skipped. Missing a few dates was a cheap price to pay to avoid all the uncertainty, fear, and heartache that must have come before and in between them. When he saw her next to him wearing her engagement ring and wedding band, he knew he had made the right decision.

With this watch, I will never have to face uncertainty again, he thought to himself. *I will know exactly where I am and what I am doing. I truly have the most extraordinary gift in the world.*

And so when it came time to worry about more serious things—like changing jobs, or moving cities, or raising children—the man knew exactly what to do. He turned the hand on his clock and—poof!—any uncertainty he had disappeared. He never had another tough decision to make. With the magical watch, all his problems became his past.

With a few more turns, the man grew up and grew old with the love of his life. At some point, they bought a house. At some point, they adopted a dog. At some point, they raised two kids. At some point, the kids left for college and got jobs.

One Thanksgiving, when the whole family was together for the first time in five years, both kids jokingly wished for time to go faster: they had found partners they loved and wanted to get married soon and start families of their own. So the man turned forward time again, this time for their sake. He did what he thought any good father would do, which was to remove all the uncertainty and confusion his children had and give them the answers they sought. Ten years flew by. At the next Thanksgiving, he realized he had grandchildren.

The last time the man used his magical watch was to avoid a trip to the hospital. His wife had suffered a stroke, and he was desperate to bring her back home as soon as possible. When he reached for his wrist, he noticed how wrinkled his hands were, how they now shook with a slight tremor. He hesitated a moment before turning the hand forward. When his wife materialized beside him, resting peacefully in bed, he felt a shock of relief. He also felt pleased. Ever since he had put on his magical watch, the man never had to endure a sad day in his life. *This is how life should be*, he thought as he stroked his wife's hair.

The ordinary man knew he was an old man now, and with a slight cough in his chest and pain in his joints, he felt it was too risky to use the watch anymore. He took it off and put it away, and he vowed he would spend every day of the rest of his life dancing with the frail woman lying next to him, just like he had on the night she was just the girl of his dreams.

But when the man woke up the next day, the woman did not. She had passed away peacefully in her sleep. The man called for the doctors, but there was nothing they could do except carry his wife away. The doctors did their best to console him. "Sir," they said, "she must have lived a long and wonderful life."

After they left, the man sat on the floor and began to weep. He wailed to the heavens and begged the angel to turn back time again, but the angel did not reply. The man ran to the drawer where he hid his watch and took it out. He sat on his bed with the watch on his wrist, winding the hour hand back again and again. Of course, nothing happened.

The man felt every emotion he had skipped over the years come crashing down all at once. It was almost unbearable, the pain, loss, agony, and grief he felt for the first time in decades. The man was horrified at what he had done. He had first used the watch because he knew life was not worth living without her. Now, she was gone again. Somewhere in between all those decades, he had fallen in love with her, raised a family with her, grown old with her. But he could not for the life of him remember how all of it had happened. The last full memory was of that night decades ago when they danced. He wished more than anything to return to that day.

That night, the man closed his eyes and made his second wish.

"Please, angel, if you can hear me, please turn back time again to the night I met my wife. I was selfish to have cheated time. I now realize I want to live through it all—the apprehension, the worry, the fear, the pain, the anger, the loss, the heartache and heartbreak—I want to know what they feel like so that I can live life like an ordinary man—to its fullest. Please, please, grant me this wish, and I will never ask to see the future again."

The man prayed and prayed until he could pray no longer, and then he closed his eyes and went to sleep.

For a long time after my mom told me this story, I wanted to be the man with the magical watch. I wanted to know what was so special about the last year of high school. I wanted to know where I would end up for college. I wanted to know who my lifelong friends would be, who my lifelong partner would be, how we would all meet and why. I also wanted to know what happened after college, what happened after marriage, what happened after kids, then grandkids, then retirement, then death. Before these events even occurred, I was convinced they would be the most important moments in my life. Everything else was secondary—moments to be forgotten, and thus time worth skipping.

That was before I lived through some of these moments and everything in between.

I still remember the day I locked myself in the creative writing classroom in high school because I was terrified to be wearing an NYU T-shirt on college T-shirt day. I had disappointed my parents already by not following my sister to Harvard; what would other people think of me? Of course, this was before I realized no one cared about me as much as I thought they did. I needed rejection to teach that truth to me—to convince me I need not worry about avoiding failure because everyone else was too busy worrying about themselves.

I also remember that my teacher at the time, Mrs. Weissenstein, was there in the classroom with me. I was crying so hard I could not speak, so she did all the talking for me.

She reached over and held my arm, and she told me I was an oak tree with a thick stem and sturdy roots reaching far and deep. No matter how hard it rained or snowed or how many people came over to trim my leaves, I had time to grow again. She told me that at the moment, I was a tree with a few stems that had fallen, but if I just trusted in time and in nature, I would understand that "this too shall pass."

I felt silly at the time, crying over such a cliché. But Mrs. Weissenstein was right—that day did pass. So did the summer months after that. So did four years of college after that.

Now, when I think back to college T-shirt day, about how terrified I was to go to NYU, I laugh. I ended up at a school I never saw myself attending, but I know that, if I had to go back and relive college, I would choose NYU again and again. My time there passed by too quickly—as it probably would have if I had gone anywhere else—and every moment had been worth living if only because nothing could be relived again.

Most people would agree that anticipation for an event feels longer than the event itself, but even so, they are inevitably shocked when things feel instantaneous anyway. I certainly felt that way attending my first Fourth of July celebration in New York City: I spent the whole afternoon walking along the East River highway and wading through the impatient crowds to find the best spot from which to watch the fireworks. I stood sweating in the heat for what felt like years; the fireworks exploding over the Brooklyn Bridge lasted only ten minutes. Looking back, I remember only about ten seconds. The past is like that—a firework show, a short-lived spectacle of fiery sparks and blooming smoke and frenzied noise I now wish I could replay again and again.

No matter how much time I spend thinking about growing up, I still cannot explain everything that has happened to me thus far. My essays are proof of this: they are drawn-out attempts to write my way into the truth without ever landing on it. In many essays, there are moments in which I cannot pin down a reason for why something happened. So I move on by making reasons up. This practice allows me to turn scattered moments into stories, to spin my narrative thread in a way that makes sense to me.

And after twenty-one years of living, what has finally begun to make sense is that the most unexpected and difficult moments in life are the ones that shape it. Rejection, loss, grief—these feelings are powerful if only because they make their jubilant counterparts feel that much more intense.

A few months ago, I called Vivian Giang, a senior staff editor for *The New York Times* and an adjunct professor at NYU, to discuss with her my work on this collection of personal essays. I spent most of the call convincing her—and myself—that after spending several months reflecting on such an unpredictable past, I was no longer worried about the hazy future.

"At this moment, I feel like I'm living through one of life's most uncertain periods," I told her. "I have no idea what I'll be doing with my life five, ten, twenty years later, but I'm writing this book to convince myself that that's okay."

"That's certainly an admirable way of looking at things."

"Well, I guess it's just nice to imagine I've figured out what growing up means. What it means to let go of my neurotic tendencies for a second and actually trust that things will work out ... eventually."

"That's good to hear," she laughed. "I hope you keep that optimism. Because to me, uncertainty only gets magnified as you get older."

Not that I do not believe her, but with only twenty-one years lived and hopefully many more to go, I am in no rush to find out whether she is right or not. With so much uncertainty to grapple with from just two decades of living, I am content to live all the questions now. I do not need answers yet; they will come in due time. The only answer I know and need now is this:

I am no man with a magical watch. For the rest of my life, I will try to take my time.

"In the end, story-truth is only marginally a function of what actually is or what actually was. Each of those dearly loved stories, like all wondrous works of art, presents us with the gift of life's ambiguity, the gift of participation without a guide dog, the gift of fleeting clarity amid overwhelming uncertainty, and the gift of encountering other lives just as random and murky as our own."

—TIM O'BRIEN,

DAD'S MAYBE BOOK

"Age is a privilege. Not everyone gets to grow old. Cherish it."

—ANNA AKANA,

SO MUCH I WANT TO TELL YOU

ACKNOWLEDGMENTS

——

This book, first and foremost, belongs to my family. While book writing is solitary work, it is also, in many cases, a family affair. More than my parents and older sister know, I drew on their support to complete this project during an unexpected year in quarantine.

Mom and Dad, I still remember the day I told you both I wanted to write a book. I was still in high school then, and you both had laughed, asking if I was being serious or if this was another fanciful dream of mine. To which I responded, of course, that the answer was both. Fast forward six years, and you are now holding this book in your hands—my literal, physical dream come true. It goes without saying that I could not have done it without either of you, the two people who first taught me what it meant to chase dreams by running after your own. I hope to one day write a dozen more books trying to express my love for you, but this one will have to do for now. Thank you for giving me everything. This dream is for you. I hope it is the first of many.

Elaine, this book would also not have been possible without you. Thank you for being the most patient and compassionate older sister I could ask for. Despite all the shoulder biting, finger pointing, cow crying, vicious pinching, high-pitched screaming, and uncalled-for bullying I inflicted upon you during our childhood years, please know that I adored you all the while, and that if it weren't for you, I would never have turned out a decent human being in the end. Thank you for being both my foil and my role model for the past twenty-one years. Thank you for your perspective every step of the way forward. Thank you for being my best friend. For our relationship, I will be forever grateful.

To my St. John's School teachers, thank you for showing me how to find comfort, grace, and wisdom in reading and writing. Mary Lacy, thank you for teaching me that beauty in language can be found anywhere, from modern novellas to classical Latin texts. Linda Carswell, thank you for giving me the confidence to write outside the classroom, and for encouraging me to submit my first essay to Scholastic Art & Writing in ninth grade. You are the reason an essay of mine was published in Scholastic's *The Best Teen Writing of 2016* and, more importantly, the reason I have my own collection of essays today. Warren Rawson, I will never read Ernest Hemingway, Flannery O'Connor, or Tim O'Brien without thinking of you. Thank you for showing me the poignancy of symbolism and of brevity. Thank you also for our hour-long chats in your classroom, our reflections about family and education and Pokémon Go, and our friendship, which is one filled with messy doodles, dry humor, and intense honesty. Russell Hardin, thank you for being a father figure in education to me. I think often of our meals together and our conversations not only about history, but about what really matters in life. You have gotten me through hard times more than you know. Marty Thompson, I still cannot believe our friendship began the day you threw my seventh grade history exam into the trash can, and I threatened to hit you for it. We somehow transformed our relationship from sworn enemies to decent hiking buddies to lifelong friends now. And look how far we've come. Thank you for always being a phone call away—I am looking forward to the day we travel and hike together again. Wendy Chang, I still have the Wonder Woman figurine you got for me for Christmas in 2015. Every time I pass by it in my room, I hear your infectious giggles, I see your commanding presence, and I am reminded of how lucky I am to have crossed paths with you. And finally, Rachel Weissenstein, I would give so much in this world just to be able to take creative writing again with you. I once heard good teachers are those who do two things: teach you about everything and change your life. If that is true, then you are one of the greatest teachers I have ever had. Thank you for teaching me about essays and poems and short stories, and about all the people and lives that lived on the page. Thank you also for convincing me that hard times will always pass, and for filling me with the courage and the resilience to grow into my own little oak tree.

To my New York University and National University of Singapore professors, thank you for proving me wrong about the whole college thing. Had I gone to Harvard, I never would have met any of you. Professor Michael North, you were right—almost everything you taught in the classroom applies to my everyday life, and with this book, I took your advice, dipped my toes into the ocean, and plunged in. Professor Sharon Friedman, I went into your classroom every Wednesday afternoon filled with contentment and relief; you and all of the essayists we studied truly were my sanctuary from a hectic day, and I always remember it as such. Professor Jeffrey Younger and Matthew Statler, I would do college all over again if it meant learning from and working with you two once more, as colleagues and as friends. Professor Jessy Hsieh, I miss your abundant energy, your incredibly open office hours, and your beautiful perspective that great professions should make you feel like you're approaching infinity. Professor Simon Bowmaker, I am still in awe of your ability to remember names and faces, and I cannot wait to have that cup of coffee with you in the city one day. Professor Reima Shakeir, I will miss our hallway chats and your hugs—they truly were the best. Professor Diane Yu, I am now always thinking of how I can be a more thoughtful leader, friend, and person because of you. Thank you for all the field trips, the guest speakers, and the opportunities to speak our minds in your classroom. Professor Mark Brennan, I appreciate your love for books almost as much as I appreciate your dry humor and rare candor. Thank you for being there for me when I needed someone to talk to about the darker things, and thank you for helping me see the light. Professor Dolly Chugh, I am becoming the person I mean to be, and your book, your mentorship, and our friendship are all helping me get there. And Professor Peter Tan, Professor Cynthia Chen, and PhD candidate Satoshi Inuzuka, I rarely get to see a foreign country through the eyes of its educators; the next time I am in Singapore, I would love to meet with you again and take you out for lunch, on me.

To my early readers, thank you for your wisdom, time, and candor. Elaine Dong, Marty Thompson, Sharon Friedman, Graham Goldberg, David Kang, Michael Ligier, and Greta Li generously reviewed individual essays. Their frank feedback saved me many hours of revisions and kept me honest throughout this process. Others who kindly shared their time and insights include Katherine Center, Aya Tanaka,

Robert Diyanni, Brandon Posivak, Carole Sprunk, Haley Newlin, Josh Lasky, Jon-Erik Jardine, Kyra Ann Dawkins, and Mackenzie Finklea.

To my friends, thank you for coaxing this project along with your humor, insight, and encouragement. Caitlyn Lubas, our Zoom-ba sessions were the only reason I stayed mildly active these past few months, and our daily calls kept me sane. Catherine Pham, your surprise coffee delivery, your kind card, your infectious enthusiasm, and your unbridled laughter kept me going on the nights I felt like I wanted to give up. Amber Liu, your surprise appearances at my house were like birthday presents to me. Kevin Zhang, Saswata Gupta, Angie Chen, David Kang, and Ryu Kurosawa, you all were my home away from home, and our Sunday evening game nights were always the highlight of my weeks. Joshua Terpstra, your random motivational GIFs and incredible music playlists were always entertaining and heartwarming. Nisarg Patel and Jesse Gan, our virtual work sessions and Netflix parties were second only to the times all three of us chatted together for hours. Evan Zhang, your jokes and sporadic company were the reason for many pleasant nights' sleep. Stella Ji, Kelly Sue-Fan, Alice Wang, Elizabeth Xu, Rebecca Stone, and Zein Tao, your enduring presence in my life as my second family has been as therapeutic and delightful as it was when we were all still kids performing together at Stafford Centre. Gabe Malek and Chris Zimmerman, our neighborhood walks gave my summer a sense of stability amidst the unexpected quarantine. Nived Gopakumar, our conversations never failed to make me both laugh uncontrollably and think deeply. Austin Gregory, your check-ins on my sanity as well as your periodic updates on your new rollerblading hobby kept me going at my own. Lauren Jhin,

Kate Porterfield, Andres Gomez Perry, Kester Tay, Su Yan Tan, Christine Chin, and Ashane Govind, our calls always brightened my day. And last but certainly not least, Peter Lee, your daily presence in my life during this tumultuous year has been my lifeboat. Thank you for making this period of isolation during a global pandemic feel a little less lonely, a little more hopeful, and a lot more loving.

To Eric Koester, Brian Bies, Gjorgji Pejkovski, Stojan Velichkov, Katie Sigler, and Emily Price of New Degree Press, thank you all for your invaluable guidance on my book from inception to publication. I am humbled and honored to have had each of you on my team as mentors, publishers, designers, and editors. Eric, you are living proof that one serendipitous phone call changes everything. Brian, our conversations shaped my vision for how I wanted to think and talk about my book for years to come. Gjorgji and Stojan, your patient expertise kept me from falling into a constant state of indecision during the cover design process. Katie, your candid guidance on my earliest drafts ultimately shaped my favorite essays in this collection. Emily, your energy as an editor was infectious, as was your willingness to share random duck facts and pictures with me over the course of many months. They got me through many late nights.

And finally, to everyone who preordered a copy of *Twenty-One Years Young* and supported me on this journey, thank you, from the bottom of my heart, for helping me make my dream into a reality.

Jennifer Adams
Yo Akiyama
Ahmed Al-Hassan
Khayre Ali
Austin Allday
Haroon Alli
John Almiranez
Jillian Amadi
Monica An
Paula Angus
Elise Anthony
Slavi Arnaudov
Adrian Azari
Shahryar Bachani
Marci Bahr
Steven Ban
Stefanie Barton
Benjamin Belfort
Misako Benso
Elly Berge
Alice Berlin
Maya Bhandari
Shivi Bhatnagar
Anurag Birla
Jay Bisda
Jay-k Bisda
Joshua Bone
Nandaki Bonthu
Simon Bowmaker
Jonathan Bujak
Ashley Cagle
Sophie Caldwell

Sebastian Camacho
Siena Canales
Anthony Cao
Linda Carswell
Sarah Cartwright
Gordon and Katherine Center
Olivia Chan
Justin Chan
Zack Chan
Wendy Chang
Sophia Chang
April Chang
Marina Chang
Shehzad Charania
Anna Chen
Michelle Chen
Jay Chen
Haiyun Chen
Jo Chen
Sheryl Chen
Christal Chen
Nancy Cheng
Sydney Cheng
Elliot Cheung
Tej Chilukuri
Christine Chin
Anusha Chintalapati
Robert Cho
Brandon Chong
Geenie Choy
Dolly Chugh
Christian Claus

Sophie Clayton
Maddie Clayton
Gian Clementi
Owen Coats-Thomas
Lauryl Cookson
Mikayla Copper
Sofia Cortez
Michael Crawbuck
Catherine Dai
Alan Dai
Elyzamarie Damaso
Lynn Dang
Corrina Daskalakis
Kurt Davies
Eric Delgado
Saransh Desai-Chowdhry
Ryder Desenberg
Ruchi Dhandhukia
Xavier Diaz
Arianna DiGregorio
Barbara DiPaolo
Lauren Directo
Robert DiYanni
Elaine Dong
James Dong
Jessica Dong
Kathleen Dunlap
Brittny Efendy
Danielle Elmers
Dominique Enriquez
Sadman Fahmid
Kelly Sue-Fan

Gordon Fang
Emily Feng
Mackenzie Finklea
Grace Firestone
Roma Forest
Joseph Foudy
Sharon Friedman
Ryan Friedman
Daniel Friedman
Jesse Gan
Gail Gant
Carl Gao
Ellice Gao
Amanda Gao
Sophie Gershenwald
Vivian Giang
Peyton Gibner
Hannah Goh
Graham Goldberg
Andres Gomez Perry
Lucy Gong
Natasha Gonzalez
Nived Gopakumar
Ashane Govind
Austin Gregory
Lori Grossman
Emily Gu
Stephanie Guo
Saswata Gupta
Jessy Hsieh
Leah Hampton
Terrie Hanscom

Rebecca Hao
Russell Hardin
Frances Hellums
Cara Henderson
Noel Higgason
Bob Hipp
James Ho
Sunny Ho
Benjamin Hon
Ashley Hong
Emma Hood
HanhLinh HoTran
Alex Hu
Janet Huang
Simon Huang
Michelle Huang
Laura and Sophia Huang
Michael Huang
Marvin Huang
Wilson Hui
Bodhi Hwang
Emily Hwang
Connie Hwang
Subah Imami
Kendra Ing
Satoshi Inuzuka
Chiemi Ip
Elizabeth Ivanecky
Courtney Jacobs
Martha Jamail
Jon-Erik Jardine
Richa Jatia

Pamela Jew
Stella Ji
Ashley Jia
Anlan Jiang
Jenny Jiang
Ava Jiang
Jacob Jiao
Berkelee Jimenez
Gracie Jing
Reiko Johnson
Jeremy Johnson
Janee Johnson
Anson Kahng
Amy Kang
William Kang
David Kang
Isabel Karohl
Kem Kemp
James Kho
Jennifer Kim
Khang Kim
John Kim
Christine Kim
Grace Kim
Jamie Kim
Shamir Kishinchand
Jonathan Ko
Eric Koester
Neha Kukreja
Ryu Kurosawa
Ethan Kwan
Lily Lau

Dara Ladjevardian

Clemence Lai

Isabel Lai

Nathaniel Lam

Ethan Lan

Feng Lan

Josh Lasky

Winnie Lau

Rebecca Leakey

Susanna Lee

Alice Lee

Youran Lee

Sylvia Lee

Jeremiah Lee

Aidan Lee

Peter Lee

Kangqiao Lei

Belinda Lei

Maura Leichliter

Chelsea Li

Cheryl Li

Wilbur Li

Danting Li

Vivian Li

Yang Li

Greta Li

Nathan Li

Belinda Li

Cat Li

East Li

Jennifer Li

Charlie Liang

Nicholas Liao

Kaiqing Liew

Michael Ligier

Isabelle Lim

Anna Lin

Joyce Lin

Tiffany Lin

Joanne Lin

Jane Lin

Jeff Lin

Ruth Ling

Pamela Liou

Conrad Liu

Anna Liu

Gina Liu

Crystal Liu

Amber Liu

Andrew Loh

Kimbery Lord

Carl Louis

Winnie Lu

Caitlyn Lubas

Dylan Luong

Regina Lustre

Louise Malek

Mohan Malhotra

Destine Manson

Ana Martinez

John McGovern

Lola McIntosh

Elizabeth McNeely

Ian Mellor-Crummey

KP Mendoza
Grace Meng
Joseph Meyer
Kelli Mijares
Elizabeth Moore
Colton Morgan
Christie Nakajima
David Nathan
Michelle Nawrocki
Haley Newlin
Nicole Ng
Cara Nguyen
Minh-Anh Nguyen
Esther Nguyen
Andrew Nguyen
Minh Nguyen
Duyen Nguyen
Dorothy Nie
Michael North
Bobbie Oldfield
Daniel Pai
Justin Pak
Jasmine Pan
Mikey Panganiban
Nisarg Patel
Maria Patterson
Danilo Perez
Catherine Pham
Tiffany Piloco
Ellen Pluta
Sandra Poh
Kate Porterfield

Brandon Posivak
Emily Price
Lana Pulgar
Eric Qiu
Pablo Querubin
Emaad Raghib
Sahitya Rajesh
Apoorva Ramesh
Dwight Raulston
Paritosh Raval
Warren Rawson
Abhinav Reddy
Sara Reddy
Yuming Ren
Amy Ren
Celina Resoso
Harriet Reynolds
Hayoung Roh
Christina Ru
Rachel Rub
Kristian Ruegg
Kristen Santiago
Milan Saxena
Sam Schneider
Brian Seam
Kimm and Katy Shafer
Reima Shakeir
Timothy Shaker
Austin Shakiban
Amanda Shang
Nisha Shankar
Simmi Sharma

Douglas Sharp
Megan Shen
Rachel Shen
Annie Shen
Jonathan Shih
Amy Shih
Philip Shin
Shaquille Sinclair
Justin Sinprasith
Stephanie Sison
Melinda Sloan
Joseph Soliman
Debra Somers
Jiayi Song
Keshav Sota
Madison Spinelli
Carole Sprunk
Rebecca Stone
Carol Sugimoto
Anviti Suri
Charlie Sutherby
Sonsera Sze
Su Yan Tan
Peter Tan
Emily Tan
Aya Tanaka
Rhea Tanamala
Jennifer Tang
Christian Tanja
Zein Tao
Namar Tarabzoni
Nellie Taratorin

Kyle Tau
Caroline Taverna
Jing Hui Tay
Kester Tay
Fanghui Teng
Julia Termulo
Joshua Terpstra
Marty Thompson
Kev To
Joseph Tolonen
Rachel Tong
Serra Topalismailoglu
Carolyn Tran-Math
Margaret Trautner
Christina Tso
Nikki Tucci
Greg Umali
Simmi Uppaladadium
Michael VerMeulen
Alice Wang
Weilun Wang
Elizabeth Wang
Eileen Wang
David Wang
Jennifer Wang
Rita Wang
Alyssa Wei
Rachel Weissenstein
Johnny Weng
Robert Whitelaw
Jordan Wolken
Kara Wollmers

Brian Wong
Marvin Wong
Sophie Worscheh
Joy Wu
Kathy Wu
Kevin Wu
Alice Wu
Juliana Wu
Kristy Wu
Alice Wu
Shirley Xu
Elizabeth Xu
Tanya Xu
Yifei Yan
Lauren Yang
Leo Yang
Jiahong Yang
Karen Yang
Suzanna Yang
Michelle Yang
Karen Yeung
Megan Yit
Christine Yoe
Joseph Yoo
Ran Yoo
Jeffrey Younger
Connie Yu
Linda Yu
Elina Yu

Grace Yu
Kenneth Yu
Lisa Yu
Lo-Hua Yuan
Liane Yuan
Raymond Yuan
Peter Yun
Francis Zhan
Mike Zhang
Cindy Zhang
Kevin Zhang
Richard Zhang
Mike Zhang
Andrew "Taco" Zhang
Evan Zhang
Margaret Zhang
Patricia Zhang
Matthew Zhang
Grant Zhao
Tina Zhao
Claire Zheng
Kaitlyn Zheng
Le Minh Zhong
Angela Zhou
Sarah Zhu
Jackie Zhu
David Ziemnicki
Christopher Zimmerman

APPENDIX

—

INTRODUCTION

Didion, Joan. *The Year of Magical Thinking.* New York: Vintage Books, 2005.

Lopate, Phillip. "Introduction." In *The Art of the Personal Essay: An Anthology from the Classical Era to the Present.* Edited by Phillip Lopate, xxiii-liv. New York: Anchor Books, 1995.

Montaigne, Michel de. "Of Experience." In *The Complete Essays.* Edited by M. A. Screech, 1207-1270. New York: Penguin Press, 1993.

O'Brien, Tim. *Dad's Maybe Book.* New York: Houghton Mifflin, 2019.

"SO IT GOES"

Vonnegut, Kurt. *Slaughterhouse-Five.* New York: Dial Press, 2009.

"OYSTER OMELETS IN SINGAPORE"

Chu, Jon M., dir. *Crazy Rich Asians.* Burbank, CA: Warner Bros. Home Entertainment, 2018. Film.

"MY MOTHER VOTED FOR TRUMP"

The Atlantic. "The Lawsuits of Donald Trump. March 20, 2013. https://www.theatlantic.com/national/archive/2013/03/the-lawsuits-of-donald-trump/273819.

BBC. "Data leak reveals how China 'brainwashes' Uighurs in prison camps." November 24, 2019. https://www.bbc.com/news/world-asia-china-50511063.

Bond, Shannon, and Avie Schneider. NPR. "Trump Threatens To Shut Down Social Media After Twitter Adds Warning To His Tweets." May 27, 2020. https://www.npr.org/2020/05/27/863011399/trump-threatens-to-shut-down-social-media-after-twitter-adds-warning-on-his-tweet.

Locker, Melissa. *Time.* "John Oliver Takes on Donald Trump on *Last Week Tonight*." February 29, 2016. https://time.com/4240734/john-oliver-donald-trump-last-week-tonight/.

Slotkin, Jason. NPR. "NYC Poison Control Sees Uptick In Calls After Trump's Disinfectant Comments." April 25, 2020. https://www.npr.org/sections/coronavirus-live-updates/2020/04/25/845015236/nyc-poison-control-sees-uptick-in-calls-after-trumps-disinfectant-comments.

"IT TAKES A VILLAGE"

Edwardes, Brittany. "Short Term Volunteer Abroad Programs & Mission Trips (1 Week & 2 Weeks)." Volunteer Forever. " February 11, 2020. https://www.volunteerforever.com/article_post/short-term-volunteer-abroad-programs-mission-trips-1-week-2-weeks/.

New York University Stern School of Business. "SIV: Social Entrepreneurship in Ghana." Stern Around the World. Accessed August 15, 2020. https://www.stern.nyu.edu/portal-partners/current-students/undergraduate/study-away/short-term-immersions/international-volunteers.

"MR. BODDINGTON'S FIVE-YEAR MEMORY BOOK"

Didion, Joan. "On Keeping a Notebook." In *Slouching Towards Bethlehem*, 131-141. New York: Farrar, Straus and Giroux, 1968.

Kafka, Franz. *Letters to Friends, Family and Editors.* Translated by Richard and Clara Winston. New York: Schocken Books, 1977.

"TWENTY-ONE YEARS YOUNG"

Alexander, Elizabeth. *In the Light of the World.* New York: Grand Central Publishing, 2016.

Sedaris, David. "The Comey Memo." In *Calypso,* 252. New York: Little, Brown and Company, 2018.

"WHEN WE STOP BEING IMMORTAL"

Accad, Michel, MD. "A Guide to Top Medical Journals: A Primer for Healthcare Journalists." Alert and Oriented (blog). April 6, 2016. http://alertandoriented.com/a-guide-to-top-medical-journals/.

Gawande, Atul. *Being Mortal: Medicine and What Matters in the End.* New York: Picador, 2014.

Made in the USA
Middletown, DE
20 August 2021